S0-AHO-700

THE DICKENS WORLD

THE
DICKENS WORLD

BY

HUMPHRY HOUSE

SECOND EDITION

OXFORD UNIVERSITY PRESS
LONDON   OXFORD   NEW YORK

Oxford University Press

LONDON OXFORD NEW YORK

GLASGOW TORONTO MELBOURNE WELLINGTON

CAPE TOWN IBADAN NAIROBI DAR ES SALAAM LUSAKA ADDIS ABABA

DELHI BOMBAY CALCUTTA MADRAS KARACHI LAHORE DACCA

KUALA LUMPUR SINGAPORE HONG KONG TOKYO

ISBN 0 19 281002 2

First published by Oxford University Press, London, 1941
Second edition 1942
Reprinted 1950
First published as an Oxford University Press paperback, 1960
and reprinted in 1961, 1965, 1969, 1971, *and* 1976

Printed in Great Britain by
Fletcher & Son Ltd, Norwich

PREFACE TO THE SECOND EDITION

THE reprinting of this book makes it possible to say a few things which should have been said before. The book would never have appeared at all but for the admirable work of Mr. Johnstone-Wilson of the British Museum, who corrected the proofs and checked or supplied a number of references during very difficult times: it owes a great deal to the advice and criticism of Mr. John Sparrow and Mr. D. P. Walker.

The first completed typescript went to America and never came back. An imperfect carbon copy was completed and corrected without reference books, in odd moments 'after duty'; and from this the text was set up. Chapters I and VII badly need rearrangement, but for many reasons, both on the publishers' side and on my own, it has not been possible to make any major alterations: a few slips have been put right, a few sentences re-shaped, and a note has been added or altered here and there to make a point clearer. Otherwise the text must stand with no addition but my thanks for the generosity with which friends improved and strangers received it.

HUMPHRY HOUSE

IN THE FIELD
    April 1942

CONTENTS

INTRODUCTION

MANY people still read Dickens for his records and criticism of social abuses, as if he were a great historian or a great reformer. Any history, of course, is a splendid field for benevolence and love of justice and indignation; for there they require no action, no awkward politics: but history which is both truth and fiction too, dressed up with caricatures and jokes, set in every kind of devised excitement and pathos, allows uplifting emotions to play upon the past with a freedom that no professed historian could decently encourage. Dickens's novels are now historical documents of this kind; and many readers who would be bored by the reports of the Poor Law Commissioners or Garratt's *Suggestions for a Reform of the Proceedings in Chancery* can look in *Oliver Twist* and *Bleak House* for pictures of their times, and contributions to the cure of the evils they describe.

In addition to this, few English novelists have been treated with such respect by the professional historians themselves. He is quoted often as indicating the trend of opinion and taste, but also on matters of fact, not merely because his familiar words will give extra point to an illustration from another source, but because his words are so often the best illustration to be had. And as history filters down from original researchers and creative historians through the various strata of text-books, references to Dickens become more frequent (one might add more careless), and of proportionately greater importance. The extreme is reached in one of the most popular History Text-Books for children between the ages of 11 and 14; the whole introductory chapter to the nineteenth century is given to Dickens, starting with a portrait and a short biography. The

novels are then quoted to illustrate the following
things: debtors' prisons, child-labour, street-boys,
workhouses, gas-lighting, London traffic and fogs, the
new police force, the Courts of Law, Government
offices, country carts, stage-coaches, inns, nursing,
railways, parliamentary elections, and education. These
various topics are held together by this paragraph:

> The great novelist, like others of his time, was a reformer.
> His stories, whether sad or humorous, often served as a
> protest against the abuses of the social and political life of
> his time. As we read the following chapters, we shall see
> how many of the abuses against which Dickens protested
> were gradually removed during the nineteenth century and
> afterwards.

Dickens history is inseparable from Dickens reformism.
That paragraph is a good example of the mild complacency which often accompanies and even accentu-
ates an interest in Dickens's exposure of past abuses:
self-congratulation harmonizes only too easily with the
Christmas spirit. Debtors are no longer jailed; money-
lenders are more strictly supervised; and a parish-boy
who asks for more can be sent to a clinic for analysis.
Good as the old days were, the new are in some ways
better, and Dickens helped to make them so. But while
it is generally accepted that Dickens did a great deal
of good, there is a genial vagueness about what exactly
he did and how he did it. It is easy to smile when a
foreign propagandist quotes Mr. Squeers as a typical
modern English schoolmaster, but it is not so easy to
say what was exactly the point of Dickens's satire in
the early part of *Oliver Twist*.

Several English writers (apart from the general
critics like Gissing and Chesterton) have dealt with
this question of Dickens's history and reformism; but,
they have nearly all interpreted Dickens more through
their own beliefs than through the beliefs of his time.

Mr. Edwin Pugh in *Charles Dickens, Apostle of the People*, published in 1908, set out, with great sense and knowledge, to show the socialist implications of his work; Mr. T. A. Jackson's *Charles Dickens: The Progress of a Radical* (1937) argues that at his death he was all but a Marxian Communist, and so on. But only M. Cazamian's *Le Roman Social en Angleterre 1830–1850* attempts in any detail to show Dickens's social and political writing in connexion with its contemporary setting of ideas; and by some accident it seems as if this book has not affected English writers as much as it might have done.

'Dickensian' scholarship—a unique accretion for an English author—is in one sense or another largely historical. It is concerned to identify persons and places in the novels and stories, to discover 'originals'. The proper interest of such discoveries is only in their relevance either to Dickens's own biography or to the social history behind his novels: and in recent years nearly all the most valuable work has been biographical.

The novels themselves are, of course, a primary source for the life. Charles Dickens was the child of Mr. Micawber (with a touch of Dorrit) and Mrs. Nickleby. He lodged for a time with Mrs. Pipchin. As a youth he fell in love with Dora, who grew up into Flora. For the biographer such identifications as these are of the greatest value; for we know more about John Dickens from *David Copperfield*, and more about Mrs. Winter from *Little Dorrit*, than from any other source. But the interest of a writer not concerned with personal biography depends upon the fullness of knowledge that other sources can give, so that he may trace the process of imaginative transformation from the supposed original to the fiction. For him, Mr. Micawber is less important than Harold Skimpole. But Dickens never wrote a *roman à clef*.

The *roman à clef* proper deals with public characters,

11

and the best examples of it in Victorian literature are Disraeli's; but his imagination was as different from Dickens's as it could be. The mistake he made in *Lothair* would have been utterly impossible for Dickens. The character of Mgr. Catesby was so closely based on a fashionable priest of the 'sixties named Capel that in one place Disraeli actually wrote Capel instead of Catesby, and the mistake was published in the edition of 1870, Vol. III, p. 254. He was so using his memory of a living man that in the moment of writing he could forget the thin disguise. Dickens's method was exactly the opposite; instead of speaking about real people as if they were fictions, he spoke about his fictions as if they were real people. We can often watch in his letters the characters growing under his hands. Leigh Hunt, no doubt, gave him the seed of Skimpole, but a great deal else was grafted on to what sprang from it, and the interest in a detailed study of the case would be to see how the grafting was done.

With Dickens, the more exact identifications are often less interesting than the more imperfect; and the historical value of those characters whom he himself admitted to be based on actual people or who have been tracked down by later research may lie least in the points of detail that suggest the 'originals'. A good deal of Squeers was Stone, of the Cheeryble Brothers the Grants, of Merdle Sadleir; but the historical value of the originals is something less than the historical value of what Dickens made of them. In this sense even mistaken identifications may become important. For instance, the writer who first suggested that Mrs. Jellyby was taken from Harriet Martineau was probably wrong; but the mistake had fruitful sense in it.

The topographical interests of Dickensians are sometimes less easy to understand. One editor of *Little Dorrit*, for example, after mentioning Merdle and 'the Sadlier (*sic*) affair' adds, 'However, the allusion, whatever

it was, is of no interest nowadays,' yet he goes on to
write pages of detailed chat about all the streets and
houses and churches mentioned in the book as if their
interest were incontestable. Topographical scholarship
and guesswork have long been surprisingly persistent
and popular. Merely looking along my own shelves I
can see these titles: *Dickens's London, The London of
Charles Dickens, Dickensian Inns and Taverns, In Kent
with Charles Dickens, The Kent of Dickens, A Week's
Tramp in Dickens Land.* In the Centenary Year, 1912,
Thos. Cook & Son ran a 'Whole day drive in Dickens'
London' every Thursday during the summer: 'Inclu-
sive Fare, Providing Table d'Hôte Luncheon at City
Restaurant, Tea at Hampstead, all Admission Fees and
Gratuities, and Services of Guide-Lecturer through-
out, 15*s*., $3.60,' and a day tour to Canterbury and
Rochester for a guinea. Even now, various branches
of the Dickens Fellowship organize 'Rambles' every
season.

The most curious instance of the passion for localizing
is the small half-timbered house in Portsmouth Street
off Kingsway, which still protests to the world that it
is the Old Curiosity Shop immortalized by Charles
Dickens, though he plainly said that *his* shop was
pulled down over a hundred years ago; it was pulled
down before the end of the novel. There would not be
money in this fiction unless customers still wanted to
believe it.

This topographical inquisitiveness has done a great
deal to stabilize a quite misleading conception of what
was the Dickens 'period'. Nearly all the energy and
ingenuity is devoted to hunting out the buildings which
were already old when Dickens wrote about them.
Inns, churches, old houses like Mrs. Clennam's and
the curiosity shop, the Inns of Court, Rochester Castle,
Tellson's Bank—these are the usual objects of the
indefatigable tourist and sightseer. But what of the

railway stations and viaducts and suburban villas and new hotels? Did Dickens live entirely in a world of reminiscence, and utterly fail to assimilate for imaginative purposes the prodigious changes that were taking place in every detail of the world he lived in; or did he wilfully reject them?

This book will attempt to show in a broad and simple way the connexion between what Dickens wrote and the times in which he wrote it, between his reformism and some of the things he wanted reformed, between the attitude to life shown in his books and the society in which he lived. It will be concerned a good deal with facts, and illustrated with quotations from miscellaneous sources; for it is only in such details that a writer's environment can be seen and his purposes understood; the exact language of contemporaries alone can have the authentic tone and idiom necessary to conviction. With an author so variously and intricately wound into the history of his time the working of his imagination can often best be seen from others' views of the events with which he started. And Dickens himself is far more factual than might appear; the best commentaries on many parts of his novels are his own articles and short stories, and articles and stories that he supervised as editor. So there will be many quotations from his minor works and from his own journals, *Household Words* and *All the Year Round*.[1]

A survey of this kind is hampered by the extremely technical nature of much that should be included in it. To be understood thoroughly Dickens should be followed into many different by-ways of history where only professional specialists can safely tread; two such by-ways will not be entered in this book. The details

[1] In the cheaper editions the Minor Works are reprinted in such various selections and rearrangements that it has seemed best not to attempt to give references to any volume: references are therefore given only to the periodical in which the essay first appeared. Complete sets of *Household Words* and *All the Year Round* can still be bought for a few shillings.

of Dickens's treatment of the Law cannot safely be discussed by any one who is not a trained lawyer;[1] his treatment of schools and education will be omitted because, for various reasons, it has been impossible to collect the necessary material.

For some years past, criticism—and more particularly what is called 'Literary History'—has been becoming more sociological. It is a truism, which no critic has ever doubted, that a great writer is a product of the social forces of the time in which he lives, and that he also reflects and modifies them in his work. To say so much is to say little more than that 'literature is inseparable from life'—the stale caution with which every literary scholar for the past century has prefaced his clinical analyses. Literature is inseparable from life, he says, but let us look at certain aspects of it. As detailed knowledge accumulates and is departmentalized, these 'aspects' become further removed, each from each, and all from the general history of the time. The emphasis of literary history has shifted from 'influences' traced as a kind of genealogical descent from one major writer to another, to biography which seeks out sources of creation in the psychological details of each writer's life; and it is shifting now again to the social and economic environment in which particular works have been produced. This recent shift is illustrated in the *Introductions to English Literature* by Professor Bonamy Dobree and Miss Edith Batho. Their volume *The Victorians and After* (1938) contains a great deal that is extremely relevant to this book, but one specific judgement on Dickens needs a separate comment:

The pity is that this giant never grew up intellectually. . . . Where Dickens touched upon social reform, anywhere in fact where he began to think, he falls below the level of the

[1] Sir William Holdsworth's *Charles Dickens as a Legal Historian* is the best book on the subject.

second-rate, though the generous indignation that he shows
is worthy of a full and complete man.

It is proper to ask whether, if it is true that his
treatment of social reform is immature and lacking in
thought, it may not be one of the main duties of
historical criticism to try to explain why it was so.
Whether it is true or not, the fact remains that an
immense number of his contemporaries—not all of them
fools by the standards of the time—took his reformism
seriously; and immense numbers after him—perhaps
not all so wise—have continued to do so. Criticism of
this kind, if it is to explain a period, has to account
for its failures and mistakes.

The word 'Dickens' in the title of this book is used
as an adjective, as when somebody says he has had a
Dickens Christmas. What that conveys varies very
widely indeed according to the taste and reading of
those who hear it: but popularly it suggests a frosty
morning; coaches; delightful inn at the end of the stage;
portly landlord; smiling barmaid; brandy by the fireside; smoking joints; good time for all. Hard upon these
Pickwick items follow mixed impressions of poverty
and good cheer and tears of happiness from the *Christmas Books*. To call a man a Dickens person would
popularly mean that he was of the Pickwick-Fezziwig-
Cheeryble type. The old coaching days, inns, and fat
humorous, benevolent men are the main features
exploited with so little mercy when any publican or
shopkeeper or collector for charity decides to work up
a Dickens spirit. Here is the verdict of Mrs. Baillie
Saunders, authoress of *The Philosophy of Dickens*
(Glaisher, 1905):

People say now as often as ever of a neighbourhood, or a
room, 'How Dickens it looks,' or 'Do not alter your house,
it is so Dickens.' I have heard over and over again, 'He
is such a dear old fellow—he is so Dickens.' Things need

no further explanation than this. It conveys a definition unmatched by the most careful description. And perhaps its most wonderful feature is its insidious spirit of kindness —you cannot be angry with anyone you call 'so Dickens'. I have never known a single instance of such a possibility.

This conception of the Dickens atmosphere is the first thing to look into.

CHAPTER I

HISTORY

'In these times of ours, though concerning the exact year there is no need to be precise . . .'

First words of *Our Mutual Friend*

THE first thing to notice in the popular conception of what 'Dickens' means is that it contains so little that is typical of the years in which most of Charles Dickens's work was done. The England for which he wrote was the country of the early railways, ruled by the Ten-Pound Householders of the first Reform Bill: yet the inns and coaches, and gaiters and brass buttons are now carefully preserved in coloured prints because they represent the world as it was before the railways revolutionized our habits and our landscape. 'The "coaching days" from Waterloo to *Pickwick*,' says Professor Trevelyan, 'still stand in popular imagination for the last era of "old England", jovial, self-reliant, matter-of-fact, but still as full of romance, colour, character and incident as the world of Chaucer's pilgrims who rode so slowly along the green tracks so many centuries before.'[1] And it is with these that 'Dickens' has come to be associated. Charles Dickens fully realized this, and when friends whom he wanted to entertain in a marked, dramatic way (they were often Americans) came to Gad's Hill, he himself became a Dickensian. He used to turn out 'a couple of postilions in the old red jacket of the old red royal Dover road',[2] and drive them round to cathedral, castle, old houses, and Kentish orchards in unremitting

[1] *British History in the Nineteenth Century*, ed. 1928, p. 167.
[2] Letter to J. T. Fields, July 7th, 1868; this particular performance was to entertain Longfellow. Among the English people for whom he did the same were Lytton, Layard the traveller, and Arthur Helps.

sightseeing.   He thought it was 'like a holiday ride in
England fifty years ago'; but what with staring shopkeepers and cheering urchins, with perhaps a Deputy
or two, it must have been more like an outing of the
Dickens Fellowship fifty years later.

In his minor works, too, he was apt to ruminate
upon the departed glories. The Uncommercial Traveller
returned to Dullborough,

> from which I departed when I was a child, and which I did
> not revisit until I was a man. . . . As I left Dullborough in
> the days when there were no railroads in the land, I left
> it in a stage-coach. . . . The coach that had carried me
> away, was melodiously called Timpson's Blue-eyed Maid,
> and belonged to Timpson, at the coach-office up-street; the
> locomotive engine that had brought me back was called
> severely No. 97, and belonged to S.E.R., and was spitting
> ashes and hot water over the blighted ground. . . . Pickford
> had come and knocked Timpson's down.[1]

The original title of the essay from which these
sentences are taken was *Associations of Childhood*; and
that title might well do service for many of his books:
in story after story he returned to Dullborough. When
his fortune was made he went back to live near Rochester
under an almost fatalistic impulse; and his last novel
was set in the place where his father's fortunes first
drooped.

He consciously created 'Dickens Land'. Rochester
was disguised as Great Winglebury, Mudfog,[2] Dullborough, and Cloisterham; it appears anonymously as
the birthplace of Scrooge and as the Market Town in
Great Expectations; it appears under its own name in
Pickwick, *Copperfield*, and *The Seven Poor Travellers*.
Dickens made deliberate pilgrimages to the district

---

[1] *All the Year Round*, Vol. 3, p. 274. 1860.
[2] In the original—*Bentley's Miscellany*, February 1837—Oliver Twist's workhouse was at Mudfog; and Bleak House was first going to be at Rochester instead
of near St. Albans.

before he went to live at Gad's Hill, and he often chose
to make them on such marked occasions in his life as
his honeymoon and his birthday.

For they were really pilgrimages in time and not
in space: he was visiting his youth. When an old
Rochester greengrocer heard his reminiscences merely
with 'a sarcastic kind of complacency', he walked away
disappointed:

> I had no right, I reflected, to be angry with the greengrocer
> for his want of interest, I was nothing to him; whereas he
> was the town, the cathedral, the bridge, the river, my child-
> hood, and a large slice of my life, to me.

Quite apart from the use he made of the Rochester-
Chatham district in his books, he was so filled with
memories of it that he came to believe that as a boy
he had lived there a good deal longer than he really
had. He told Wilkie Collins in a letter on June 6th,
1856: 'I was taken . . . to Chatham when I was very
young, and lived and was educated there till I was
twelve or thirteen, I suppose.' In fact he lived there
most probably from 1816, when he was four, to 1823,
when he was ten.

The ten years following, spent in London, at the
blacking-factory, at school, as a lawyers' office-boy, as
a reporter in the Courts, were almost as important.
His father's imprisonment in the Marshalsea and the
work of gumming on labels were branded on his memory
by shame: *David Copperfield* and *Little Dorrit* are
peculiarly the books of those years. But there is hardly
a story which is not directly touched by them. Then
he was learning the by-ways and slums of London;
the intricacies of lawyers and the absurdities of their
clerks; the full meaning of 'shabby-genteel'; the ways
of landladies and lodgers; the social pretensions of
obscure men; the use of money; the sins of poverty; the
value of ugliness; the love of death. It is astonishing,

with a writer of Dickens's fertility and scope, to see how his first book, the *Sketches*, forms a prospectus of what he was to do for the next thirty years.

There is no need to emphasize any more that he used the years of his youth with a persistence and confident exactness unequalled by any other writer whose youth was not, like Proust's, his one chosen subject. This truth recurs throughout Forster's biography, and has been reiterated by all biographers since. The years between 1816, when he was four, and 1836, when he began to be successful, could bring his imagination to a state of such intense creative excitement that he was sometimes tempted to draw on that time mechanically when other capital failed; or else in a moment of hesitation a scrap would shoot up from his memory and bring a whole dull page to life. Even the names of characters come from the tombstones in Cooling churchyard and from the petty-cash book he kept in his second job as an office-boy.

This continued habit of drawing on his own past is of the greatest importance to anybody who wants to treat Dickens's books as historical documents, or to see them in relation to their age; for it meant that he tended to push his stories back in time so that the imaginary date was a good deal earlier than the date of writing. He had no exact historic sense, no desire to make his stories into accurate 'period' records, and no particular fear of anachronisms. The stories often contain material which keeps the original colour of several different periods in his own experience; they also bring together widely spaced material that can be checked by outside evidence. But though he had little historic sense, he had a very acute sense of time; he liked to give his books a surface of tidiness and punctuality; he went out of his way to indicate precise dates and seasons of the year, and sometimes even used known historical facts to enforce the actuality of a moment. But in the next chapter he might use a second fact quite incompatible with the first. To condemn these mistakes as anachronisms would be to impute a consistent historical purpose that he never had. But it would be absurd to treat them on the principles of Vivian, in Wilde's *The Decay of Lying*, as something to boast of. 'There is such a thing,' he says, 'as robbing a story of its reality by trying to make it too true.' Dickens had all the love of documentation that Vivian decries in the realists of the later Victorian age; the Preface to *Nicholas Nickleby* stresses not only that the facts about Yorkshire schools are even something below the truth, but also that the Cheerybles really existed. It is not the genuineness of a document or a memory that spoils or makes a book, but the way it is used. Dickens so far admitted the principle that a novelist's facts should be right, that he sometimes let himself be led into defending his mistakes.

A simple mistake occurred at the beginning of *Pickwick*. The book was written 1836–7, and announced plainly in the first chapter that its action was supposed to begin in 1827; in the second, Mr. Jingle claimed to have written an 'epic poem—ten thousand lines— revolution of July—composed it on the spot—Mars by day, Apollo by night,—bang the field-piece, twang the lyre'. The slip was later covered by a facetious footnote: 'A remarkable instance of the prophetic force of Mr. Jingle's imagination; this dialogue occurring in the year 1827, and the Revolution in 1830.' This, and the mistake over 'Burked',[1] were significant slips to have made in an early exercise in thinking back.

Pickwick, being nearest to the great impressionable years, has their experience squandered on it in grand disorder: it is thus a vast playground for Dickensian scholars. They have made plain enough that numbers of its incidents fit exactly in letter and in spirit the

[1] Burke, the strangler, was executed in 1829.

imaginary years of the Pickwick Club's life, and that Dickens writing, in 1836, about 1827, used a great deal of matter directly from his own experience of nine years before. Lowten, the clerks at the Magpie and Stump, and the office-boys in their first surtouts, come from the time when he worked for Ellis and Blackmore—then, too, he had his chance of studying Mr. Justice Gaselee for the future Mr. Justice Stareleigh, and of watching Mrs. Ann Ellis in an eating-house near Doctors' Commons for signs of Mrs. Bardell. The choice of 1827 for his story made it possible to use many detailed memories without having to adjust them at all.

We need not now join the scholars at their alley tors and commoneys, or follow them in any minute identifications: but it is worth seeing what lies behind the popular love of the *Pickwick* coaches and why Dickens himself shared it. For they have a special place in the Dickens historical scheme.

Though horses and coaches are the necessary machinery of the quick changes of scene, the journeys and chases and accidents which link the story so unmistakably to the picaresque novel of the eighteenth century (and, in a different way, to the sporting sketches which Dickens was originally meant to imitate), all the means and details of travel have an importance which such things never had for Fielding or Smollett.

The shadow of the railway falls in *Pickwick* only on the heading to Chapter VIII; scarcely anybody could then have foreseen that before long the coaches would be off the road for good. To an Englishman of 1836 the coach-system of his time was a portent of speed, efficiency, and innovation. Within the memory of a man of forty, the coaches and roads had improved beyond belief; and they were still improving. Dickens knew what the changes meant. If we compare the scorn with which, at the beginning of *A Tale of Two Cities*, he treated travelling on the Dover Road in 1775 with

23

his delight in Mr. Weller's driving down to Ipswich, we see the full effect of Palmer and Macadam and the pride men had in progress before the railways made progress a commonplace.

The coaching atmosphere of Pickwick is concentrated in the character of Mr. Weller senior; but contemporary critics thought Weller out of date even for 1827. *The Quarterly Review* for October 1837 fastened on him as one of Dickens's grand mistakes. In the first place, said the reviewer, his portrait was plagiarized from Washington Irving's *Sketch Book* and spoilt in the process. The charge of borrowing is at least reasonable. But the point of the criticism does not lie there alone; for the article goes on:

> The fact is, the old race of coachmen were going out when Mr. Washington Irving first visited England, and were altogether gone before Mr. Dickens's time. The modern race are more addicted to tea[1] than beer; the cumbrous many-caped great-coat is rapidly giving way to the Mackintosh; and, with the change of habits and the increase of numbers, they have been doomed to see their authority over stable-boys and their awe-inspiring influence over country people pass away. . . . Mr. Dickens failed, therefore, because he had never seen what he pretended to describe.

Irving was first in this country in 1805, seven years before Dickens was born, when Palmer's Mail Coaches were still comparatively new. Improvements in the mails and privately owned coaches followed slowly; there was no sudden leap to the efficiency of the 'thirties. This was largely because the roads, which were worse in England in the early part of the century than in Scotland, made rapid improvements in coach-design and time-tables impossible. The Reports of the Select Committees on Highways and Turnpike Trusts of 1819,

---

[1] Others said coffee: cf. 'Coachmen of science and respectability can alone be employed. In fact, to the increased pace of their coaches is the improvement in these men's moral character to be attributed. They have not time now for drinking. . . ." *Quarterly*, December 1832.

before which both Telford and Macadam gave evidence, show what old Weller must once have been used to. In a working life of, say, twenty-five years, he had seen great changes. Dickens even made some allowance for this in the story Sam tells about his father in Chapter XIII:

'It's a werry bad road between this and London', says the gen'l'm'n.
'Here and there it *is* a heavy road,' says my father.

In 1827 the changes in roads and coaches, and coachmen's ways, were not nearly so far advanced as when the *Quarterly* reviewer wrote. But still Weller, with the atmosphere that depends on him, falls between two worlds: he is even a hybrid between two types of men, the casual roisterer and the prompt, efficient, public servant. His easygoing ways and everlasting drinking are hardly consistent with his precision about way-bills and loads, punctuality and speed. We need not decide whether he had one or more originals:[1] it is enough to see how Dickens in creating him combined details and atmosphere typical of his own boyhood, or even of a time before it, with a modern pride in the achievements of the age.

The boys of Dickens's generation were coach-conscious as their predecessors had never been. Power over speed and efficiency of movement was then first becoming a focus of childish admiration: boys were ambitious to be coachmen, as later to be engine-drivers. They haunted the White Horse Cellar in Piccadilly and the General Post Office to see the coaches, as they afterwards hung about King's Cross to see the streamlined engine of the Flying Scotsman.

[1] Mrs. Lynn Linton's attempt to identify him with 'Old Chumley' who drove the London-Rochester coach in the 'thirties is interesting, because when she made it she couldn't have known that Dickens had any connexion with Rochester; but it proves nothing, for after *Pickwick's* success people must have been distorting coachmen everywhere into Weller's likeness.

But the boys who were boys between Trafalgar and *Pickwick* suffered from a stroke of history such as did not disturb their successors in the next hundred years. For they saw the beautiful and impressive object of their childish love replaced by a rival whose aesthetic qualities were of a quite different order. A young man of 1836, whose earlier ambition had focused on the box seat of the Birmingham Mail, found it very difficult to transfer the thrill and glamour to the footplate of an engine on the London and Birmingham Railway: he was too old. By the sudden development of this new means of travel such a man had become *laudator temporis acti* before middle age, and he lived on without the possibility of disillusionment about his boyish dreams.

'Coaching' has thus become idealized in popular memory not merely as a striking and picturesque feature of a vanished world, but because a whole generation, in which were many writers, caught by admiration of the coaches in their short-lived pride, was unable to work off in the boredom of adult experience the glamorous ambitions of boyhood.[1] 'The old coaching days' are largely the literary creation of Dickens, De Quincey, and Tom Hughes. It is often said that Dickens never really grew up: in this respect the course of history made it hard for him to do so.

[1] cf. T. A. Trollope: *What I Remember*, 1887, Vol. I, page 32. 'A journey on the box of the mail was a great delight to me in those days—days somewhere in the third decade of the century; and faith! I believe would be still, if there were any mails available for the purpose.' If the mails *had* continued he would almost certainly have come in time to prefer the comparative comfort of an inside place. The Introduction to *Felix Holt* (1866) is also very relevant. Dickens himself noted in the 'sixties that pictures of coaches in a hotel were of damaged and ruinous survivals from the earlier days; the retrospective cult of coaching prints had not yet begun (*The Uncommercial Traveller*, Ch. XXIV). Angus B. Reach in *The Railway Note-Book* (1852) had picked out among the admirers of 'the good old coaching days' the old-fashioned farmer and the horsy young swell; he then went on: 'Occasionally, on railways and in society, but more frequently in books, you listen to the sentiments of a more refined lover of the olden times—of a gentleman and a scholar somehow affected with that moral squint which makes people look round the corners of centuries and ogle lovingly that which has passed utterly away. Often the sentiment is pressed as much in joke as earnest. . . .' Such were the people still living partly in their boyhood.

It is, of course, from *Pickwick*, and most of all from the coaching parts of it, that the popular idea of the Dickens 'period' is mainly derived; but the time-strands in the book are so various that the period they suggest is an imaginary one: retrospection and ante-dating combine to produce an amalgamation for which the supposed date is little more than a convenient label. With *Pickwick* itself the motive for ante-dating was probably mere expedience: it made it easier for Dickens to use his best and most vivid material if he pushed things back nine years, but the experience was still too close to be deeply coloured by the mood of imaginative reminiscence that is best seen in the earlier parts of *David Copperfield* and *Great Expectations*. In these two books at least the ante-dating seems a matter of internal compulsion.

But other considerations led to the same result in others of the novels: Dickens was enough of a pure story-teller to want to answer the child's insistent question, 'What happened next?'; he could hardly leave a book without tracing the lives of the main characters over the next five or ten years after the proper climax of its plot; if there has been a marriage there must be children, and they must grow up enough to talk to the repentant grandfather or to play on the grave of the dead cousin; if there has been a lovers' separation there must be a decent interval abroad before the forced reunion; the rescued must have time to prove that they have really made good; even the good must have an appendix in which to be true to themselves. It is always something of a shock to remember that Mr. Dombey lived on into an affectionate old age, or that at the end of *The Old Curiosity Shop* Kit Nubbles was a father.

These summaries of family history in the final chapters must never be taken too literally. It would scarcely be possible to work out backwards an exact and consistent chronology for a single one of the novels. *David Copperfield* and *Great Expectations* are the most clearly planned, and yet in each there is a hurried telescoping at the end. But, broadly speaking, Dickens allowed for his endings, and made his beginnings early on purpose. In the last paragraph Mr. Pickwick is spoken of in the present tense.

Of the few novels which are explicitly dated, *Little Dorrit* best shows the more serious later consequences of the urge back to the past which is so marked already in *Pickwick*. The first part came out at Christmas-time, 1855, and, like *Pickwick*, announced at the very start that it was a story of the eighteen-twenties:

> Thirty years ago, Marseilles lay burning in the sun one day.
> A blazing sun upon a fierce August day . . .

and later in the book this dating is kept to:

> Here lie the mortal remains of JOHN CHIVERY, Never anything worth mentioning, Who died about the end of the year one thousand eight hundred and twenty-six . . .

All the details of the Marshalsea are taken from memories of the time (1822) when John Dickens was imprisoned there; and Dickens only went back to look at the half-demolished prison after *Little Dorrit* was finished. His amazement then was not at finding his memory so accurate, but at seeing the ruins so true to his memory.

In the greater part of its detail *Little Dorrit* remains faithful to its imagined date: yet two of its outstanding themes derive not from memories of the past, but from the topical events of the time in which it was written. It is well known that the satire on Government Departments as the Circumlocution Office was directly prompted by the administrative muddles of the

Crimean War; yet this satire was grafted on to a story of the middle twenties. The character of Merdle, too, was a deliberate transference. Dickens did not publicly commit himself to saying who was his original: 'If I might make so bold,' he said in the later Preface, 'as to defend that extravagant conception, Mr. Merdle, I would hint that it originated after the Railroad-share epoch, in the times of a certain Irish bank, and of one or two other equally laudable enterprises.' John Sadleir, the Tipperary banker, failed and committed suicide in 1856. Dickens had the general idea of Society courting a newly rich man before that: but he privately told Forster that he 'shaped Mr. Merdle himself out of that precious rascality'. Suggestions of Hudson the Railway King and Sadleir need not on any personal grounds raise the cry of anachronism; but it is important that all the parts of the book in which Merdle appears are a satire on social and financial conditions which belong more truly to the crisis of the late 'forties than to that of the middle 'twenties, with which they are apparently meant to be connected.

These examples suggest a provisional rule which is useful in assessing the historical importance of the novels—not less useful because there are exceptions to it. It is this: that whatever may be the imaginary date of the plot, the material most likely to be contemporary with the time of writing, and most topical to it, is the 'Reformism' and the more deliberate social satire.[1] This does not mean that there may not be other contemporary material besides, but that the urge to treat contemporary things is moral and reformist rather than emotional, pictorial, and dramatic.

It is so often said in a loose and general way that Dickens's books were one of the great reforming forces

[1] e.g. *Pickwick*, Chapter XV, belongs peculiarly to the 'thirties. For contemporary evidence of lion-hunting see, for instance—*a*) Harriet Martineau: *London and Westminster Review*, April 1839; *b*) Carlyle: *Sir Walter Scott, London and Westminster Review* No. 12, 1838; *c*) Anon: *The New Monthly Magazine*, 1837, Pt. II, p. 175.

of the Victorian age that we are apt to treat them too freely as reliable source books for the history of the abuses which were reformed away. But it is quite impossible to treat them so without sorting out some of their chronological tangles. To do this thoroughly for every book would be impossible; even to make the attempt would take more space than can be spared here. But one example given in some detail will show the method which underlies the later chapters of this book. No novel is better for the purpose than *Bleak House*, because so much depends on its treatment of the Court of Chancery, and because it has all the usual problems, in an acute form.

Bleak House was published in monthly parts from March 1852 to September 1853, and Dickens seems to have gone out of his way to leave the imaginary time of the story vague. When Esther copies into her narrative the letter in the wonderful legal jargon of Kenge and Carboy, she deliberately says: 'I omit the date.' No year is given anywhere, and there is scarcely even the name of a month. This is more surprising because the sense of the passage of time is so peculiarly vivid, and makes more impression on the memory, perhaps, than the chronology of any of the novels. This powerful imaginative effect is produced by term succeeding vacation and vacation succeeding term in the Court of Chancery, and by the changes of the seasons down at Chesney Wold. But the tempo of events in the two main strands of the plot is curiously dissimilar. If we isolate the Jarndyce theme from the Dedlock theme, we think of Richard Carstone's failure, entanglement, and decay as slow and long-drawn-out, but of the events which hurried Lady Dedlock to discovery and death as a swiftly moving series of crises. Yet on the whole the two are meant to synchronize: Lady Dedlock does not die many pages before Ada discloses her pregnancy; and the story proper has then less than nine months to run. And at the end, as so often with Dickens, even what should be slow is hurried.

By watching the seasons and the terms it might appear that from Esther's first going to Bleak House to the death of Richard was something just less than three years. But at several points the time-table is congested and obscure, and John Jarndyce himself suggests that it is probably wrong. The main story cannot have happened later than 1843–6, and is also assumed to be much earlier.

The personal experience on which Dickens was drawing when he described Guppy and Jobling clearly belonged to the same years which produced Lowten and the 'Magpie and Stump'; that is, to 1827–31, the period between leaving school and becoming a reporter in the Gallery of the House of Commons. During this time he was seen to be reporting cases in the Lord Chancellor's Court, and the Lord Chancellor from 1827 to 1830 was Lord Lyndhurst.[1] But Lyndhurst was Chancellor again in 1834, and for a third time from 1841 to 1846. So, even if we boldly say that he was the Chancellor of *Bleak House*, it proves very little about the date of Caddy's marriage or the dispute between Coodle and Doodle.

But, dotted about in the book, there are other quite clear indications of time—all rather contradictory, though they seem to be so definite. One of the most unexpected is the sudden statement in Chapter XLIII that Harold Skimpole 'lived in a place called the Polygon, in Somers Town, where there were at that time a number of poor Spanish refugees walking about in cloaks, smoking little paper cigars'. Their identity

---

[1] Holdsworth in *Charles Dickens as a Legal Historian* accepts the Lyndhurst identification from Atlay's *Lives of the Victorian Chancellors*, Chapter I, p. 143, but goes on (p. 79): 'If it be true that the Lord Chancellor described in the third chapter of *Bleak House* is Lord Lyndhurst, the time at which the action of the story takes place must be taken to be in or about 1827, when he was made Chancellor in succession to Lord Eldon.'

is plain enough: they were the 'group of fifty or a hundred stately tragic figures, in proud threadbare cloaks' described by Carlyle in his *Life of John Sterling*, the exiles of the Torrijos party, well known round St. Pancras between 1823 and 1830, whom Dickens must often have seen as a boy. But their picturesque irruption into *Bleak House* hardly tallies with the landscape measured and broken for the coming railway out of Lincolnshire (Chapter LV). The scorn with which the shining hatted and belted policeman looks down on the beadle (Chapter XI) as 'a remnant of the barbarous watchmen-times' suggests a superiority in the 'Peelers' not acquired too soon after 1829. Mr. Bucket, too, belongs very much to the reformed world.[1] Mrs. Pardiggle's Puseyism, and the Carlyle-like attack on the latest dandyism (Chapter XII), which seems to mean partly the Oxford Movement and partly Young England, would, taken by themselves, commit the story at least to the later 'thirties. Mr. Turveydrop seems to have maintained his lonely deportment for some years since the death of George IV. Mrs. Jellyby and all her works belong, as we shall see, in spirit and in detail to the 'forties. And one of the originals for Jo was almost certainly a boy called George Ruby, 'who appeared about fourteen years of age' when he was called at the Guildhall on January 8, 1850, to give evidence in a case of assault.

> *Alderman Humphery:* Well, do you know what you are about? Do you know what an oath is?
> *Boy:* No.
> *Alderman:* Can you read?
> *Boy:* No.
> *Alderman:* Do you ever say your prayers?
> *Boy:* No, never.
> *Alderman:* Do you know what prayers are?
> *Boy:* No.

[1] The C.I.D. had its origin in the plain-clothes detectives first appointed by Sir James Graham, Home Secretary, in 1844: see below p. 202.

Alderman: Do you know what God is?
Boy: No.
Alderman: Do you know what the devil is?
Boy: I've heard of the devil, but I don't know him.
Alderman: What do you know?
Boy: I knows how to sweep the crossings.
Alderman: And that's all?
Boy: That's all. I sweeps a crossing.[1]

These things are of varying importance; but if we try
to fix a precise date to the story, some at least of them
must be misplaced. It seems unlikely that even
Dickens, careless as he was, would have brought to life
such marked and dated people as Mrs. Pardiggle, Mrs.
Jellyby, and Inspector Bucket, in a world that could
not possibly have known them. It is quite possible
that when Esther wrote the last section of her narrative
'full seven years' after the story proper was ended, she
wrote at the same time as Dickens, in 1853; which
would mean that Richard died in about 1846, and that
the story probably began in the early 'forties. But the
whole atmosphere of the legal parts of the book and
numbers of the small details—the Spanish exiles among
them—are drawn out of the inexhaustible store of
memories from Dickens's early days.

Overlaid on this confusion of the past was a reformist's anger with the immediate present. Both the Court
of Chancery and the slums were topical subjects in
1852, for other reasons than because Dickens made
them so. People were then in fact dying of litigation
and of cholera. It is on the relation between this
topicality and the material from other dates that we
must focus, if we want to find its historical interest.

It is quite impossible to say that *Bleak House* has
any predominating and consistent historical 'atmosphere': others of the novels can be dated with more

[1] Dickens almost certainly read these exact words, as they are taken from *The
Household Narrative*, January 1850, the monthly supplement to *Household Words*.

confidence—*Oliver Twist* is intensely topical to the time of its publication; *Our Mutual Friend* rejects a precise date, but is a modern story of the 'sixties; the main mood of *Dombey and Son* is of the 'forties, though the book's scheme of chronology tries to push it farther back; *Edwin Drood* seems to belong to the 'fifties— twenty years, or rather less, before it was written. *Nicholas Nickleby, The Old Curiosity Shop*, and *Martin Chuzzlewit*, all indeterminate and obscure, are oddly erratic in their tone. *Hard Times* is a sport and an anomaly. The two of Dickens's novels which can least be read for historical reasons are *Barnaby Rudge* and *A Tale of Two Cities*. Yet even they have a special interest, because they show what he, in 1841 and 1859, was thinking about the past.

His interest in the remote past was either pictorial or moral, and the two were not divided. It is curious that he, who was so scornful of the moral abuses of the times in which he lived, should have almost universally condemned the times before him. There is no trace of idealizing the past. When he writes of the Middle Ages, or even of the late eighteenth century, he does so with an amused contempt for their standards of life, which shows him as a proud Victorian, conscious of living in a progressive age. He treats knights-in-armour as if the knights, as well as the armour, should have ended their days in a junk-shop. The church in which Little Nell at last finds rest is a monstrous curio rather than the relic of a great civilization. It is a fit place for the vague dreams and fears of a tired child: there is not a hint that the lonely hours she spends there, amidst muddle and neglect, are so quiet because the place has lost all its original dignity and purpose. By a sort of historical table-turning she extracts consolation from the tombs: the doctrine which promotes her happiness exudes fortuitously from the stones. The forms of its present teaching by the 'simple-hearted old gentleman, of a shrinking, subdued spirit' are not mentioned, and the forms of its past teaching are not recalled. The building is more a mausoleum than a sanctuary. So Durdles treats Cloisterham Cathedral as so much stone to be sounded with his hammer for the old 'uns.

In *A Tale of Two Cities* (Chapter II) the description of the coach-journey from London to Dover is a picturesque catalogue of discomfort and risk, prepared for by a general introductory essay on the coarseness, cruelties, and dangers of 'the year of Our Lord one thousand seven hundred and seventy-five'. Dickens used the past, in fact, as an additional field for his genius in describing the unpleasant: the Gordon Riots and the French Revolution were unpleasant on a panoramic scale. Among the false book-backs with which he decorated his study at Gad's Hill was a set called: 'The Wisdom of our Ancestors—I. Ignorance. II. Superstition. III. The Block. IV. The Stake. V. The Rack. VI. Dirt. VII. Disease.' The voice of the Ten-Pound Householders could hardly speak more plainly. It was the voice, too, of Bentham, who had called 'Our Wise Ancestors', 'the Wisdom of our Ancestors', 'the Wisdom of Ages', and 'the Wisdom of Old Times', mischievous and absurd fallacies springing from the grossest perversion of the meaning of words.

CHAPTER II

BENEVOLENCE

SIR HENRY MAINE was, I think, the first to link Dickens with Bentham:

'It does not seem to me,' he wrote in *Popular Government*, 'a fantastic assertion that the ideas of one of the great novelists of the last generation may be traced to Bentham. . . . Dickens, who spent his early manhood among the politicians of 1832 trained in Bentham's school, hardly ever wrote a novel without attacking an abuse. The procedure of the Court of Chancery and of the Ecclesiastical Courts, the delays of the Public Offices, the costliness of divorce, the state of the dwellings of the poor, and the condition of the cheap schools in the North of England, furnished him with what he seemed to consider, in all sincerity, the true moral of a series of fictions.'

This suggestion was taken up by Dicey,[1] who accepted it without criticism; but he used it as a step in his argument that the Benthamite individualism of the 'thirties was already being abandoned in the 'fifties by those who had formerly held it. He took it as true that the young Dickens was a Benthamite radical; but he then quoted *Hard Times* to show that the man who was in 1846 'the editor of the organ of the Manchester school' had become by 1854 'the satirist and the censor of political economy and utilitarianism'. He took the alteration to be 'unconscious'; but a closer reading of Dickens would have reminded him that Mr. Filer appeared in 1843. For Dickens was consistently the indignant satirist and censor of the 'classical' economists; but this need not mean that he was never in

[1] *Law and Opinion in England*, 2nd edition, p. 419.

36

any sense a Benthamite. Maine's statement that 'he
spent his early manhood among the politicians of 1832
trained in Bentham's school' is literally true, but we
need to remember that he spent his early manhood also
with the politicians trained in the schools of Eldon,
Wellington, and Peel.

One of the most irritating things about Dickens's
biography is that we know so little about his work as
a reporter in the House of Commons. He must, in fact,
have attended many of the chief debates between 1832
and 1836, but it is impossible to say exactly which.
The most important pieces of legislation in those years
were the Reform Bill itself, the new Poor Law of 1834,
and the Municipal Corporations Act of 1835. He must
have been familiar with the details of argument on
both sides of all the questions that this legislation
involved: they are in fact reflected in his work. The
Eatanswill election, the ancient and loyal borough of
Muggleton, the Board of Guardians in the early chapters
of *Oliver Twist*, might, perhaps, have been described
by a man of genius who had no more than a newspaper
acquaintance with the politics of the time. But, knowing what we do about Dickens, it is reasonable to
attribute something of the confidence, not to say
cocksureness, of his satire to his Parliamentary life.
We know that he always retained a contemptuous
distaste for Parliament itself, and still more for its
parties; but it is impossible that the whole experience
of those five years should have had merely negative
results.

A very large number of the members in the first
Reformed House of Commons were influenced directly
or indirectly by Bentham's work, and it must have
been more in listening to their speeches than in any
reading that Dickens was indoctrinated with Benthamism, if at all. It would be hard to find a more truly
Benthamite joke than the curt epitome of 'The Wisdom

of Our Ancestors' quoted at the end of the last chapter:
it is a facetious summary of a whole section of *The
Book of Fallacies*; but it is quite possible that Dickens
did not know it. For so many of Bentham's ideas had
trickled down through various channels from their
source, joining minor streams of opinion from other
sources as they went, that it is quite impossible to
detect, even in writers more familiar with ideas and
arguments than Dickens ever was, what is Benthamite
and what is not.

Dickens only mentioned Bentham once in all his
written work. When the Cloisterham gossips were
talking about Neville after the disappearance of Edwin
Drood they said he had been brought to the town from
London by Mr. Honeythunder 'because that Philan-
thropist had expressly declared: "I owe it to my
fellow-creatures that he should be, in the words of
Bentham, where he is the cause of the greatest danger
to the smallest number"' (Chapter XVI). A joke on
a Benthamite catch-word proves nothing. Not everybody who was influenced by Bentham was a Benthamite: many, like Macaulay, had a great and sincere
admiration for his legal work while they disagreed
violently with his politics and ethics. Many others, who
cared little about or actively disliked his more constructive theories, were influenced both in law and
politics by the critical and destructive side of his work,
and Dickens was one of these. It is impossible to say he
disliked Bentham's theories, because there is no evidence that he knew what they were. But it is clear
that Mr. Pickwick is not Bentham's idea of a moral
man. For the Benthamite σπουδαῖος has to act from the
conviction that it is his duty to promote happiness:
Pickwick promotes it in spite of himself, almost against
his will. The man who promotes the happiness of
others in this way is in danger of being a butt;
and Pickwick starts as very little else: it is only

gradually that he begins to appear as a person to be admired rather than laughed at. John Mill said of Bentham:

> Personal affection, he well knew, is as liable to operate to the injury of third parties, and requires as much to be kept under government, as any other feeling whatever; and general philanthropy, considered as a motive influencing mankind in general, he estimated at its true value when divorced from the feeling of duty—as the very weakest and most unsteady of all feelings.
>
> [*Dissertations and Discussions*, I, 362.]

Yet the goodness of the leading Dickens moral characters, from Pickwick to Boffin, depends on just those two things—personal affection and general philanthropy. They are all good-*natured*, and seem to act as they do because they cannot act otherwise. Not one of them has a moral policy, or a considered opinion about why he does good. They seem to have no temptations, difficulties, or struggles: they are uniform, unruffled, and unreflecting.

The key to these characters is 'benevolence'. In addition to spectacles and black gaiters, Mr. Pickwick had 'a benevolent countenance': Mr. Brownlow was 'an elderly gentleman of benevolent appearance, in a bottle-green coat': it was pleasant to write down that Abel Garland and his bashful young lady reared a family, 'because any propagation of goodness and benevolence is no small addition to the aristocracy of nature, and no small subject of rejoicing for mankind at large'. It seems, in fact, as if this peculiar quality were certain to be hereditary, so much was it part of the nature of those who possessed it. The benevolent characters of the Pickwick-Brownlow-Garland-Cheeryble type are never themselves the mouthpieces of destructive Benthamite criticism: their facile charity forbids censoriousness; they are too busy being happy to think.

Such explicit criticism as is made at all is made by Dickens in his own person; nearly all the rest is done by caricature of the evils to be destroyed. This means that though the benevolent people are clearly meant to be the representatives of an improved moral order, there is often no satisfactory link between the evil and the cure. Dotheboys Hall does not break up for the last time because the Cheerybles are kind or because Nicholas is High Minded, but because it is discovered that Squeers has forged a will. Yet it is clear that in Dickens's own mind, and in that of his public, these good people were fulfilling an important social function; he had the public with him.

His popularity was never greater than in the first part of his writing life: the world then opened its arms to him, and its heart. For in all the chorus of love and praise the loudest strain was for his goodness. He himself, in the Prefaces he wrote for later editions, used to point the morals of his stories, hoping they would do some good, or lessen a wrong; and sometimes he recorded—with a faint touch of pride, as if he might himself have had a hand in the matter—that the worst evils he had described had since been remedied.

As early as 1838 the *Edinburgh Review* saluted his work as a moral force:

> One of the qualities we most admire in him is his comprehensive spirit of humanity. The tendency of his writings is to make us practically benevolent—to excite our sympathy in behalf of the aggrieved and suffering in all classes; and especially in those who are most removed from observation. . . . His humanity is plain, practical, and manly. It is quite untainted with sentimentality. . . . He is equally exempt from the meretricious cant of spurious philosophy. He never endeavours to mislead our sympathies—to pervert plain notions of right and wrong—to make vice interesting in our eyes.   [Volume 68, pp. 77–8.]

In 1845 *Douglas Jerrold's Shilling Magazine* published this *Sonnet to Charles Dickens*:

> Oh, potent wizard! painter of great skill!
>   Blending with life's realities the hues
>   Of a rich fancy; sweetest of all singers!
> Charming the public ear, and at thy will
>   Searching the soul of him thou dost amuse,
>   And the warm heart's recess, where mem'ry lingers,
> And child-like love, and sympathy, and ruth,
>   And every blessed feeling, which the world
>   Had frozen or repressed with its stern apathy
> For human suffering! 'crabbed age, and youth,'
>   And beauty, smiling tearful, turn to thee,
> Whose 'CAROL' is an allegory fine,
> The burden of whose 'CHIMES' is holy and benign.

The next year Lord Carlisle, speaking at the Manchester Athenaeum, referred to him as 'the master of our sunniest smiles and our most unselfish tears' whom 'it is impossible to read without the most ready and pliant sympathy'.

That such a poem could appear in reputable print, that a man permitted 'to bear a part in the highest councils of the State' could use such words about a young writer of thirty-four, shows something of the moral hold he had on his public. But he could never have gained it if he had been more of a pioneer. He seemed topical to thousands: he was not too topical for them to see the point, nor too advanced to have the public conscience on his side. Detached now from his time he may seem more original and adventurous than he was; for then he was only giving wider publicity in 'inimitable' form to a number of social facts and social abuses which had already been recognized if not explored before him. He shared a great deal of common experience with his public, so that it could gratefully and proudly say, 'How true!'; he so exploited his knowledge that the public recognized its master in knowing;

but he also shared with it an attitude to what they both knew, and caught exactly the tone which clarified and reinforced the public's sense of right and wrong, and flattered its moral feelings.

Dickens himself never claimed to be a pioneer: the facts he used and the abuses he attacked reached him by the same means as they had often reached his readers. The Preface to *Nicholas Nickleby* makes clear that the cruelties of Yorkshire schoolmasters were already fairly well known from newspaper reports of actions against them, and in the novel John Browdie gives a warning to Squeers:

> ''Soizes,' cried John, 'thou'd betther not talk to me o' 'Soizes. Yorkshire schools have been shown up at 'Soizes afore noo, mun, and it's a ticklish soobjact to revive, I can tell ye.' [Chapter XLII.]

Imprisonment for debt, which Dickens hammered at for over twenty years, had been attacked before he was born: his own father, after being in the Marshalsea, benefited by the Insolvent Debtors' Act of 1813; and the whole question was being loudly canvassed when *Pickwick* came out. He was often even rather behind the times. His popularity as a moralist was thus enhanced by his habitual retrospection: his ante-dated plots took some of the sting out of his satire for those who merely wanted entertainment, and encouraged the mild exercise of historical comparison for those who cared for profit and instruction. His originality was not in his moral and sociological subjects themselves, but in the fact that he conveyed familiar topics of every kind into fiction: his charity-boys and starved, half-witted drudges claimed admission to the drawing-rooms and boudoirs occupied by the handsome whiskered heroes of the Minerva Press.

When we find his contemporary critics claiming that he was not only doing something new in fiction, but even giving new information about the actual world, they must be read circumspectly. Richard Ford wrote in a very smart review of *Oliver Twist*:

> Life in London, as revealed in the pages of *Boz*, opens a new world to thousands born and bred in the same city, whose palaces overshadow their cellars—for the one half of mankind lives without knowing how the other half dies: in fact, the regions about Saffron Hill are less known to our great world than the Oxford Tracts; the inhabitants are still less . . .

But the ignorance can hardly have been blank in anybody; and thousands of people certainly knew a good deal about such places. Some time before 1820 Anthony Trollope's two elder brothers heard stories of 'sundry mysteriously wicked regions, where the bandit bands of the great city consorted and lived outlaw lives'; and they heard accounts of Saffron Hill especially, 'where it was said all the pocket handkerchiefs stolen by all the pickpockets in London were to be seen exposed in a sort of unholy market'. So the two small boys went there, thinking this extraordinary spot as remote and strange as the realms of Prester John.

> Report had spoken truly. Saffron Hill was a world of pocket-handkerchiefs. From every window and on lines stretched across the narrow street they fluttered in all the colours of the rainbow, and of all sizes and qualities. The whole lane was a long vista of pennon-like pocket-handkerchiefs!
>
> [T. A. Trollope: *What I Remember*, I, p. 11.]

The inhabitants were fairly well known too. Just as the publication of *Oliver Twist* was ending, the Evidence before the Select Committee on Metropolitan Police Offices and the Report of the Constabulary Force Commissioners showed in fuller detail than any novel could give—less stereotyped than such reports in these days —weird melodramatic facts about vagrancy and petty crime. In these and in the Reports of the Society for the Suppression of Mendicity, which had appeared annually since 1818, thieves, fences, prostitutes, lure little boys, haunt the same slums. And the slums themselves—Seven Dials, St. Giles, the Saffron Hill district —had been notorious in the cholera epidemic of 1832: even Coleridge noticed them from Highgate. Disguised as Demophilus Mudlarkiades, he wrote to be promulgated gratis an 'Address premonitory to the Sovereign People . . . for the use of the useful classes, specially of those resident in St. Giles, Bethnal Green, Saffron Hill, etc.', a jingle of facetious advice on hygiene and politics to the people who lived round Fagin's den or in Tom-all-Alone's.[1]

In making Saffron Hill the central scene of *Oliver Twist*, Dickens was thus using a contemporary topical allusion with which a great number of his readers would have been quite familiar beforehand. Its reputation was notorious, and he built on it so as to increase his own popularity. Schools for young thieves, like Fagin's, continued for many years, and one of them was described in an early number of *The Household Narrative* among the various police reports and crime stories of which the paper always had plenty.[2]

Oliver Twist provides another obvious example of the way in which Dickens revived the discussion of old abuses. There had been intermittent propaganda against the use of small boys for chimney-sweeping

[1] cf. Theodore Hook's opening to *A Day's Proceedings in a Reformed Parliament.*

[2] When a boy was on trial for theft on January 21st, 1851, a policeman described what he saw through a window. 'He saw the prisoner in a room with a line tied across it, and from this line was suspended a coat, in the pockets of which were placed pocket-handkerchiefs. A dozen little boys surrounded the prisoner, and each in turn tried his skill in removing a handkerchief without moving the coat or shaking the line. If he performed the manœuvre with skill and dexterity, he received the congratulations of the prisoner; if he did it clumsily or in such a manner as would have led to detection, had the operation been performed in the usual manner in the street, the prisoner beat them with severity, having on the occasion in question knocked down and kicked two of the boys for not having exhibited the requisite amount of tact and ingenuity in extracting the handkerchief.'—[*Household Narrative*, January 1851.]

ever since the later part of the eighteenth century: Blake's poems are now the best-known example of it. There had even been scrappy and ineffective legislation to put the chimney-sweeping business under some sort of public control. Dickens himself in one of the *Sketches* had described the wretched state of small boys, five years old perhaps, standing about helplessly in the dark and cold of early mornings waiting for the servants to let them in to their work. Exactly the same detail had appeared in Evidence before the Parliamentary Committees on Climbing Boys:

> *Q.* Did they always get in as soon as they knocked?
> *A.* No, it would be pleasant to the profession if they could.
> *Q.* How long did they wait?
> *A.* Till the servants pleased to rise.
> *Q.* How long might that be?
> *A.* According how heavy they were to sleep. . . .

And this had been public twenty years before.[1]

Of course, nothing suited Dickens better than that an evil was an old evil, that Parliament had tinkered with it and failed to cure it, that there had been a Committee of the Lords about it, that a Board or a set of Honourable Commissioners had been appointed to inquire into it and report on it, that papers about it had been through and through the Circumlocution Office, accumulating Barnacle instructions How Not To Do It. He lingered over the dying of the old Civil Service as a fond specialist in death-bed scenes; the fascination for him of anything gawky and strained extended to the growing-pains of the new administrative systems, the Heir, if not the Child, of Chaos and

---

[1] Dickens loved to describe how the old Houses of Parliament were burnt down by the fierce blaze of the Exchequer tally-sticks in the stove of the House of Lords. This happened just after a Bill had been passed forbidding sweeps to call in the streets. As the flames went up 'one of them was in a high glee because the "hact" was destroyed, and, in the joy of his heart, set up, above all the roar, the cry of "Sweep!"'

Old Night. But he could never have taken his public along with him in the reforming chase as he did in the 'thirties and 'forties, unless he had shared with it, not only familiar details which were there for all to see, but also a moral mood fairly widely diffused among those who could buy or borrow the precious numbers as they came out.

The main symptoms of Dickens benevolence are these:

(1) Generosity, in money, and in kindness that costs nothing. Both kinds of generosity are chiefly shown by the poor towards each other and by the benevolent well-to-do towards the poor.

(2) An acute feeling for suffering in all forms, whether caused by poverty, sickness, cruelty (mental or physical) or injustice. The feeling becomes most acute when all these causes of suffering are combined in the sufferer, and there is somebody who has power to relieve them all.

(3) Righteous, if ineffectual, indignation against all anomalies, abuses, and inefficiency in social organizations or government which cause suffering of any kind. This is the Benthamite strain, found more in Dickens's own words than in the words of his characters.

(4) An equable and benign temper in the benevolent person, which is on the whole immune from the changing moods which make human beings interesting in themselves.

The question is why benevolence, symptomized by such qualities as these, should have been so quickly praised and so readily provided in the best-sellers of the eighteen-thirties and eighteen-forties.

Walter Bagehot, reviewing the new collected edition of Dickens's works in the serene security of the later 'fifties, looked on such benevolence as an outmoded taste: for him it was a temporary phenomenon best explained as a reaction against the harsh and narrow spirit in high places which had been typical of the period immediately succeeding the Napoleonic wars:

> The unfeeling obtuseness [he said] of the early part of this century was to be corrected by an extreme, perhaps an excessive, sensibility to human suffering in the years which have followed. There was most adequate reason for the sentiment in its origin, and it had a great task to perform in ameliorating harsh customs and repealing dreadful penalties; but it has continued to repine at such evils long after they ceased to exist. . . . Mr. Dickens is an example both of the proper use and of the abuse of the sentiment.
>
> [*Estimations in Criticism*, II, p. 193.]

This is far too comfortable a way of looking at it; but there is a substantial truth in the statement that this sentiment was popular and even fashionable in the 'thirties and 'forties as it never was before or after. In Douglas Jerrold's play, *Bubbles of the Day* (1841), Lord Skindeep says, 'Benevolence is my foible'.

The best contemporary analysis of the public opinion which welcomed Dickens so gladly is to be found in John Mill's review[1] of Helps's *Claims of Labour*. He is dealing mainly with the question of 'improving the condition of the labouring classes'—particularly in the manufacturing districts; but he extends his range to cover the various kinds of sympathy with the poor of which Helps's book is an expression. Malthus's theory of population, he says, first turned the minds of thinking men to the problems of poverty. Though first understood as an argument for the conservative acceptance of suffering and distress, it was later seen to suggest the possibility that the whole labouring class might be improved in its condition. In any case the problems it raised were widely discussed among educated people. The crisis over Catholic Emancipation and the Reform Bill 'brought home for the first time to the existing generation a practical consciousness of living in a world

[1] *Edinburgh Review*, 1845; reprinted in *Dissertations and Discussions*, II, p. 181.

of change'. The old system had lost its *prestige*. Chartism was the expression of this change in 'the labouring portion of the Commonwealth': it strongly impressed conscientious and sympathizing minds among the ruling classes, while the threats of physical force which accompanied it compelled the attention of those who might otherwise have remained blind. This combination of ideas with outward circumstances produced a considerable literature, which played its part in extending the opinion from which it grew: Carlyle's *Chartism* and *Past and Present*, for instance, were 'an indignant remonstrance with the higher classes on their sins of omission against the lower'. Meanwhile, the investigations of the Poor Law Commission, the struggle of parties over the Corn Laws and over the condition of the factory operatives kept the deplorable details of poverty before men's minds. The feeling awakened from these many causes might be, says Mill, as influential as the anti-slavery movement if it only had as definite an object. 'The stream at present flows in a multitude of small channels. Societies for the protection of needlewomen, of governesses—associations to improve the buildings of the labouring classes, to provide them with baths, with parks and promenades have started into existence!' Schemes for shortening hours of work were discussed in Parliament, and numerous projects for relieving unemployment in the country districts. 'If these, and other modes of relieving distress, were looked upon simply in the light of ordinary charity, they would not fill the large space they do in public discussion. . . . But it is not in this spirit that the new schemes of benevolence are conceived. They are propounded as instalments of a great social reform. They are celebrated as the beginning of a new moral order, or an old order revived.' The aims and theories of such benevolence 'are not now confined to speculative men and professed philanthropists. They are familiar to every reader of newspapers, by sedulous inculcation from day to day.'

At a hundred years' distance, when we can see in better perspective all the complexities of the industrial revolution coming to a head, it is impossible not to find one of the chief causes of the new benevolence in fear. Such squalor and barbarism underlay the prosperity of Early Victorian England that, apart from the abortive rising of 1839, the possibility of revolution was rarely far from men's minds between 1834 and 1848. There was an actual class war, but there was the possibility of cholera too. The newspaper accounts of every torchlight meeting were grim reminders at the breakfast table of the pestilence that walketh in darkness: local and national reports on Public Health and Sanitation were warnings of the sickness that destroyeth in the noonday. Carlyle, in *Chartism* and *Past and Present*, is not only an angry but a frightened man. His bluster is more truly indicative of public feeling than the rhetorical panic of Macaulay's speech on the People's Charter. Every subscription to a benevolent scheme was in part an insurance premium against a revolution or an epidemic. And, further, the increasing difference between the incomes and social habits of the middle and working classes put the pleasures of doing good within the reach of greater numbers as surely as it provided a wider field for their exercise. The power to patronize is one of the most delightful consequences of going up in the world: the snobbery of a rising middle class works both more subtly and more thoroughly in its attitude to what has been left below, where the ground is known and understood, than in the upward journey, where a slip may lead to disaster or to ridicule.

Specific objects of Dickens's reformism—the relations between employer and employed and between the classes; the Poor Law; Public Health, Sanitation, and Housing; the use of Charity—will be discussed later.

In dealing with these problems he accepted none of the current curative nostrums without criticism, nor did he substitute any alternative plan of his own. He was not a Benthamite or Philosophical Radical or Chartist or Owenite or Christian Socialist or Young Englander, nor did he start a Dickens party. But he did, at least in the earlier novels, attempt to sketch a kind of human being which might become a focus of reformist sentiment. If everybody were like this, he seemed to say, the complex evils of the world would automatically be cured, the nostrums unnecessary.

In general it is true that each of the reformist parties focused upon one or two aspects of the social chaos to the exclusion of the rest, or emphasized one or two sides of human nature and minimized the importance of the others. The religiosity of Young England was as intolerable to an Owenite as the hedonistic calculus was to both. The points of the People's Charter made no appeal to anyone who, like Carlyle, regarded Parliaments with contempt. Miss Martineau would hardly be enjoyed by the public of 'Charlotte Elizabeth'.[1] Competing doctrines cancelled one another out, and the great majority of the ordinary public, giving no lasting adherence to any, was left with nothing but a sediment of vague wishes for improvement.

Dickens did not deliberately set out, after a course of sales research, to find what the public wanted. He wrote about what he wanted himself. He disliked nearly all the theories, and made most of them at one time or another the objects of his satire. His problem was to construct a general ideal of character and action which should neither make prominent those traits in human nature emphasized by any doctrinaire party, nor advocate the practical policy of any labelled group. He was not a Tolstoy: it was quite beyond his range to show in fiction a great man's struggles towards new

[1] Mrs. Tonna (previously Mrs. Phelan), *née* Charlotte Elizabeth Brown.

moral forms. Though he took a good deal else from Carlyle, he never attempted to use the idea of the superman.[1] The only other course open to him was to take the commonest and simplest sorts of human kindness and show them intensified. His good people are precluded from thought because if they once started thinking they might begin to become tendentious; their scope of action is narrow and domestic, because if it were wider they might be in danger of becoming politicians. These negative qualifications make them rather colourless and commonplace; but the members of the ancient 'party of all good men' may perhaps become effective if their goodness can appear as uniform, unshakeable, and pure. Being detached from the controversies and ambitions of the time, they must gain their moral influence by the exaggeration of qualities which are not peculiar to the time. It is the combination of detachment with exaggeration that makes these characters seem to us dreary, unctuous monsters. For we cannot now read about Pickwick in his more consciously benevolent moods, Brownlow, the Cheerybles, and Garland without some impatience: when they are not unpleasant they are tedious, and the parts they play in their plots are too mechanical. In particular, Dickens's trick of stressing peculiarities of look or manner or dress, which is so brilliantly successful in comic or grotesque figures like Pecksniff or Quilp, tends to make these benevolent old boys revert to the butt-type, from which Mr. Pickwick set out. The Cheerybles' hand-rubbing, John Jarndyce's wind-in-the-east, Boffin's trotting, perform much the same function as the gaiters for which Master Humphrey would not accept Pickwick's apologies. For us the caricaturist's themes detract too much from the dignity of what is meant to be admirable. Several of Dickens's contemporary

---

[1] Carlyle used to call him 'little Dickens', as if the adjective applied to more than his body.

critics made similar objections; some for religious or other doctrinaire reasons, others because they shared our point of view; but on the whole even these tricks were thoroughly accepted and approved, because they added humour to an ideal of personal goodness which held out some hope of escape from social anxieties without demanding adherence to an argued theory. They met the wants of those who were not 'speculative men and professed philanthropists'.

The symbol of these benevolent characters is Christmas; their attitude to life has been well called by M. Cazamian 'La Philosophie de Noël'; their aim is the all-the-year-round Christmas first recommended by Boz:

> There seems a magic in the very name of Christmas. Petty jealousies and discords are forgotten; social feelings are awakened, in bosoms to which they have long been strangers; father and son, or brother and sister, who have met and passed with averted gaze, or a look of cold recognition, for months before, proffer and return the cordial embrace, and bury their past animosities in their present happiness. Kindly hearts that have yearned towards each other, but have been withheld by false notions of pride and self-dignity, are again reunited, and all is kindness and benevolence! Would that Christmas lasted the whole year through (as it ought), and that the prejudices and passions which deform our better nature, were never called into action among those to whom they should ever be strangers.
>
> [*Sketches by Boz*, Characters, II.]

Christmas means the breakdown for a season of the restraints imposed by normal social life, a sort of psychological release, in the manner of the Saturnalia. It means release from cares that dim the affections—grandmamma unbends even to Margaret who married a poor man without her consent; it means relaxation of the formality and strictness of business relationships—you wouldn't believe how Dick and Ebenezer went at it when old Fezziwig cried, with a sharp clap of his hands: 'Let's have the shutters up before a man can say Jack Robinson!' The process of breakdown is the theme of *A Christmas Carol*: we do not know how Scrooge lost the jolly alacrity of his boyhood; but he recovered it by the destruction of all his habits and the whole framework of observation and policy he had applied to life. The experience allegorized in the journeys with the three spirits—mere pictorial allegory without any pretence of belief in supernatural power, Grace, or anything like that—implies a complete change in his values, the birth of love, and a new vision of the world.

Another writer might have probed the agony of such a conversion, lingered on the burden of the mystery, and shown the transformed Scrooge as a quiet, meditative man whose very knowledge of the truth removed him rather from his fellows, though in love. But Dickens understands nothing of such people; the loneliness of a loving character would be for him a point against it: the language of his religion is all in human metaphors, its charity is confined to the existing scheme of social life and takes its tone from common heartiness. Scrooge does not see the Eternal behind the Temporal, a new heaven and a new earth: he merely sees the old earth from a slightly different angle. His conversion, moreover, seems to be complete at a stroke, his actions after it uniform: there is no hint of his needing at intervals to recruit his strength for the new part he has to play; there are implied no periods of restlessness and despondency even, which so commonly mark the extravagantly buoyant, genial type of nature. Redlaw, the haunted man, goes through a more complex struggle, but in the end his regeneration comes about only through contact with Mrs. William, who is just another of the even, almost mechanical, fountains of good.

The Christmas spirit is not confined to the *Christmas Books*, the *Christmas Stories*, or the set descriptions of

Christmas in the novels: it is present in every attempt to hold up benevolence as a social ideal. It is obvious that at Christmas-time itself, when the love and junketing last at most two or three days, the moral adjustment is fairly easy, and derives a great deal of its force from the knowledge that it is an interlude. But how can the New View of Society for which it stands be prolonged throughout the year? Can anyone remain *exalté* for twelve months as if in the first glow of generous drunkenness? How is the spirit of generosity to be reconciled with the necessities of ordinary economic life? The religion of Christmas must have a casuistry; and in the attempt to find one, Dickens returns to those great Victorian problems—the relations between employer and employed, and the use of Charity.

CHAPTER III

ECONOMY:
DOMESTIC AND POLITICAL—I

NEARLY everybody in Dickens has a job: there is a passionate interest in what people do for a living and how they make do. The shopkeepers and land-ladies, who contribute so much to the atmosphere of close though honest business, have no monopoly of the working scene. Milliner, washerwoman, engineer, shipwright, glove-cleaner, barber, midwife, wet-nurse, waterman; actors, showmen, detectives, schoolmasters, are traced among the most surprising technical details: the stock-in-trade of Silas Wegg is minutely inven-toried; almost every moment of the time of Mortimer Lightwood's office-boy is accounted for; and the time is known when Toodle comes home for tea. The railwayman in *Mugby Junction* is so completely identi-fied with his job that he has no name but Lamps. It is the same with the professions: only the clergy marry, bury, and christen rather uneasily against a background of high pews, hassocks, and three-deckers while the pew-opener counts her tips behind the vestry door. The typical rootless, baffled person is one who, like Richard Carstone, cannot settle to a profession and make good.

Work plays an essential part in the characters' approach to life: each sees another first as a business proposition. When Ralph Nickleby has forced his way up Miss La Creevey's staircase she thinks he wants his portrait done in miniature, and he sets out to warn her that she won't get her rent. This professional view of life is most marked and constant in the lawyers: for their profession has a phrase and a fee for all the contingencies of human existence. Every remark of Mr. Jaggers implies a cross-examination: without a word his bitten forefinger implies one. Mr. Guppy's proposal to Esther is all legal jargon, the only language he understands. Wemmick forces the issue home; Walworth sentiments will not do in Little Britain; his whole private life is a piece of fantastic escapism from work,. and is therefore thoroughly controlled by it.

The characters not only talk shop, but use shop metaphors when they talk about other things:

> 'Wery good, wery good,' said Mr. Weller. 'Alvays see to the drag ven you go down hill. Is the vay-bill all clear and straight for'erd?'
>
> 'The schedule, sir,' said Pell, guessing at Mr. Weller's meaning, 'the schedule is as plain and satisfactory as pen and ink can make it.'

The moral of *Tom Tiddler's Ground* is put into the mouth of the tinker: 'that metal that rotted for want of use, had better be left to rot, and couldn't rot too soon, considering how much true metal rotted from over-use and hard service.' The story told in Dr. Marigold's patter is one of the most effective self-contained pieces of writing Dickens ever did:

> My father had been a lovely one in his time at the Cheap Jack work, as his dying observations went to prove. But I top him. I don't say it because it's myself, but because it has been universally acknowledged by all that has had the means of comparison. I have worked at it. I have measured myself against other public speakers—Members of Parliament, Platforms, Pulpits, Counsel learned in the law,—and where I have found 'em good, I have took a bit of imagination from 'em, and where I have found 'em bad, I have let 'em alone. Now I'll tell you what. I mean to go down into my grave declaring that of all the callings ill used in Great Britain, the Cheap Jack calling is the worst used. Why ain't we a profession? Why ain't we endowed with privileges? Why are we forced to take out a hawker's license, when no such thing is expected of the political hawkers?

Where's the difference betwixt us? Except that we are
Cheap Jacks and they are Dear Jacks, *I* don't see any
difference but what's in our favour.

For look here! Say it's election-time. I am on the foot-
board of my cart in the market-place. . . .

The whole flow and gusto of the writing comes directly
from the job.

At times the insistence on professional status becomes
tedious, and shows Dickens in his weakest habits,
anxious to play upon a theme. The continual soldier-
hood of George Rouncewell is bad; Mr. and Mrs. Bagnet
are worse; there are points against the sailors. But
even here there is the justification in experience that
lawyers, soldiers, sailors, and clergymen least throw off
the ways and language of their work, unless house-
keepers excel them. At other times Dickens uses a
theme to balance a job, a job to illustrate a theme.
Pecksniff's theme is hypocrisy and he is nominally an
architect: yet we know from the first that his main
income, helped out by commissions on rent, is from
the premiums of pupils who learn nothing but to
copy elevations of buildings already built, or to design
what could scarcely be built at all. Through all the
greater part of the story we are allowed to forget about
Pecksniff's profession; but at the end we see him in
all the architect's fame and pride at the opening of
a new school, of which the design was really young
Martin's. The only building we hear of Pecksniff
doing was another's. His hypocrisy and his job have
kissed each other.

Jobs, too, are used as part of the mechanism of horror
and absurdity. The dealers in death are headed by
Mr. Sowerberry, Mr. Mould, and Messrs. Omer and
Joram, Undertakers: a quick professional eye passing
over a living man can estimate the cost of his coffin
to a shilling. Those who miss a decent burial may be
rifled by Rogue Riderhood as the tide comes down

through the Pool, or be sold piecemeal to Mr. Venus for articulation. In Venus horror and absurdity compete, and it is he who has to suffer the tribulation of a choice between business and love.

This minute attention to the business of life gives Dickens's novels their immense solidity: each is a full world where the characters can fully be themselves, even doing the smallest thing. The prodigious grotesques, like Quilp or Sarah Gamp, maintain their unique life among a caste of more ordinary people because they are so carefully linked to a world of commonplace affairs, the world of moneylending and sickness and birth. The link in nearly every case is money itself. Money is a main theme of nearly every book that Dickens wrote: getting, keeping, spending, owing, bequeathing provide the intricacies of his plots; character after character is constructed round an attitude to money. Social status without it is subordinate.

In the early books finance is on the whole individualistic: businesses flourish or fail within a limited circle of customers or clients—their type is the small shop with a connexion. The good business-man is the man who starts without capital, and makes a fortune by personal virtue and industry. Companies are shady, promoted by a few unscrupulous people as an extension of already shady traffic. The United Metropolitan Improved Hot Muffin and Crumpet Baking and Punctual Delivery Company, which occupies the whole second chapter of *Nicholas Nickleby*, might well belong to the speculative rage which preceded the great crash of 1825–6, when steam-ovens, steam-laundries, and milk-and-egg companies competed with canals and railroads for the public's money.[1] The Muffin Company's

---

[1] The Muffin Company's meeting was to promote a Private Bill in Parliament: in 1825 438 petitions for such Bills were presented, and 286 Private Acts passed. See Martineau: *History of the Thirty Years' Peace*, Vol. I, pp. 355–60 (1849 edn.). There is an account of the crash of 1826 in Theodore Hook's novel *Maxwell*, where the wicked financier Apperton plays a more realistic Nickleby part.

benevolent propaganda about benefits to the human race, which made the men cheer and the women weep, is admirably true to the spirit of those progressive years. But with Ralph Nickleby on the Board neither its moral nor its financial status was much above that of the Anglo-Bengalee Disinterested Investment and Loan Company which later offered such glowing advantages to the world in the names of Montague Tigg and Jonas Chuzzlewit.

For the finance of investment has hardly become, in these early novels, a recognized system: it is rather an elaborated form of private enterprise, and the investing public is a mere flight of gulls. The typical financial business-man is not a stockbroker or jobber or company promoter or speculator, but a man who specializes in notes-of-hand, mortgages, and loans for personal expenses: he buys and sells debts. The typical money-greedy men are misers and legacy-hunters. Speculation, as with Nicholas Nickleby's father, is a form of suicide rather than a way of getting on in the world. The power of rich men is not a wide social power which, while it lasts, gives them public respect: it is direct power over individuals' lives by signed bills; its sanctions are hints of blackmail, the bailiff and the debtors' prison. Their victims' names and circumstances are on the books: they are the recording angels of spendthrifts.

Romance is valued in sterling. Pylades does not show his loyalty to Orestes in the dangers of long journeys and rescues from death, but in surreptitious loans or in sharing the last sixpence. Money is the instrument by which the villain thwarts the hero; and the two are chiefly distinguished by their attitudes towards it; their attitudes to women are secondary. Dickens points a debt at a man's head much as G. P. R. James points a pistol: his heroes are unarmed because they are poor. Money is a weapon of immense power: physical strength, passion, religion, all quail before it;

only death shows its weakness. There is hardly a story without at least one character in whom the love of money is a master humour. Grandfather Smallweed and the patriarchal Casby need hold no candles to Arthur Gride and Jonas Chuzzlewit. The series only reaches its climax in the last completed book with Fascination Fledgeby and the deceitful Boffin, who arrives with a cabful of the lives of misers to make Silas Wegg read about Daniel Dancer and Elwes.

But though Dickens himself had obviously been fascinated by such people as Dancer and Elwes, he did not create misers of the sterile and passive kind, who love money merely for its own sake, and hoard their useless coin in chimneys and teapots. His misers might be parsimonious enough to eat carrion at a pinch, but would hardly do so unless somebody felt the pinch besides themselves: they are parsimonious enough only to eat well at other people's expense, but yet do not love their own money for the sake of what it will buy. If Ralph Nickleby had merely wanted to buy a clerk he could have bought a far better one than Newman Noggs at very little more cost: but he cared too much for his power. It is the same with old Smallweed: his greatest delight is to bully from his cripple's chair a strong, brave, honest soldier. Miss Havisham, a cripple by choice, bullies her Pocket relations with an unknown will. Magwitch in the wilds of Australia gloats over his ability to make a gentleman: Pip is at his mercy.

This obsession with money's power goes to explain Dickens's lasting interest in Debtors' Prisons. His socialist admirer, Mr. Edwin Pugh, detected in this a serious 'obliquity of moral vision'. 'To the end of his life,' he wrote, 'Dickens never seemed to perceive that the creditor is, far more often than not, more to be pitied than the debtor.' He attributed this moral obliquity to 'his wholly natural sympathy with his foolish, feckless father'. But that is not enough. It is certainly true that most of the experience, visual and emotional, on which Dickens's descriptions of debtors' prisons were based came directly from the time when his father was in the Marshalsea; it is true also that imprisonment for debt was an obvious target for destructive Benthamism; but still the pity for debtors is only the extreme instance, backed by the most authentic experience, of an attitude to money which is apparent in all his treatment of it. For money is an instrument of cruelty, and imprisonment is the most spectacular form of suffering it can inflict.

Dickens has a far more acute sense of what money can do for those who have none than of what might be done with it by those who have plenty. His good rich men have no style beyond kindness, no taste beyond comfort. Patronizing the arts means being patronizing to Harold Skimpole; the get-up of Bleak House is exactly suited to the ideas of a girl like Esther Summerson. Giving security and happiness to a few people for their lifetime is more important than providing a public endowment that might last for generations. His interest in the 'haves' is almost confined to what they can do personally, good or evil, to the 'have-nots'. The proper heroes and heroines are those who suffer and are helped.

This heroizing of the underdog cannot be attributed wholly, or even mainly, to Dickens's personal experience in the narrow sense that he suffered agonies of shame for his early poverty. *Pickwick* is, on the whole, the book of a successful young humorist very pleased with his place in the world; and the next book after it, with an underdog hero, has scarcely a trace of autobiography. At the time of writing, self-identification with the parish-boy must have brought back a lot of painful feelings from childhood: but *Oliver Twist* is governed more by the acquired opinions and attitudes of adolescence and early manhood than by those.

Apart from *Hard Times* it is the nearest thing to a pure *tendenz roman* that Dickens ever wrote: its theme and tone were more suggested by what he heard in the House of Commons than by his own life or by Lytton's *Paul Clifford*. For the discussions of the Poor Law woke, by their Malthusian strictness, the wonder of the middle classes. Saffron Hill was known to be a bad place, but was it inevitably bad because of a geometrical ratio, unless paupers were to be drilled like convicts? People's minds were then focused upon the facts and problems of poverty as they had not been before, and scarcely have been again since 1850. That is why, when Dickens wanted to show his benevolent reformism in action, he started at the poor man's end. Close observation of poor people at work, at home, and laying out their wretched income, prepared the way for generous intervention.

For instance, in *The Old Curiosity Shop*, we are shown first the inner details of the Nubbles household. The whole of Chapter X—the crowded room, Mrs. Nubbles working late at her ironing, the plain food—leads up to Kit losing his job at the curiosity shop; Mrs. Nubbles

> rocked herself upon a chair, wringing her hands and weeping bitterly, but Kit made no attempt to comfort her and remained quite bewildered. The baby in the cradle woke up and cried; the boy in the clothes-basket fell over on his back with the basket upon him, and was seen no more; the mother wept louder yet and rocked faster; but Kit, insensible to all the din and tumult, remained in a state of utter stupefaction.

Kit then scours the streets for work. This all prepares for his chance meeting with Mr. Garland, coming back to 'work out the shilling', and his getting a new job with 'the kindest master that ever was or could be'.

The Cratchit family are described in all their threadbare pinching before Scrooge relieves them. The nervy anxieties of the Tetterbys, with their failing business, anticipate Mrs. William and the recovered Redlaw. The orphan Charley is caught 'managing' for the other children before John Jarndyce takes her up.

The benevolence does not work on vague material: charity meets the exactest needs. In fact, one of the reasons why Dickens's benevolent sentiment still has power to bring tears to the eyes, when literary fashion and moral taste incline so heavily against it, is that it has been so well prepared for: he has built up so carefully and realistically scenes of poverty, depression, and unhappiness that the ultimate release—the death, the £5 note, the turkey, the job, the smile—brings a break of tension also for the reader. Without such a background Benevolent Sentimentality may justly be sneered at; and we do not weep. The effect is largely got by giving a proper importance to money.

All the good characters who can afford it are great spenders: they pay good wages, lend on generous terms, give large amounts away. We are not allowed to forget that the religion of Christmas must lead to practice, or that practical benevolence needs money. Scrooge's first act after his conversion is to send for an enormous turkey and to offer the boy a shilling when he comes back with it, half a crown if it's in less than five minutes. To this day, notices in shops and pubs urging customers to 'Join Our Christmas Club' are reminders that Christmas is still as expensive as it was when Mrs. Tetterby found there was so much calculating and calculating necessary before she durst lay out a sixpence for the commonest thing. If expensive for two days, how much more so all the year round.

Pickwick does, in fact, describe an all-the-year-round Christmas. It is difficult to believe that in all the years during which Mr. Pickwick was in business he earned as much as he spent on the short adventures of his club. Argument is likely to be less about how stupid successful business-men can be than about how guileless Mr. Pickwick really was. But we no more think of vetting his bank account than of lecturing him for drinking too much milk-punch in a wheelbarrow. Yet even in *Pickwick* the money-realist Dickens is beginning to appear: there is the debtors' prison and there are the exact details of Sam Weller's screw—he found it worth his while to leave the White Hart for £12 and two suits of clothes a year, all board and travelling expenses paid. With the other novels before us we can detect in *Pickwick* one of the main problems that Dickens was always struggling with—the relation between employer and employed. The *Pickwick* standard of extravagance can hardly be kept up: there is work to do; the money must be earned.

But we notice at once that in nearly every case when Dickens showed a good employer in action there was something abnormal, even phoney, about him. When Kit Nubbles 'was formally hired at an annual income of Six Pounds, over and above his board and lodging, by Mr. and Mrs. Garland, of Abel Cottage, Finchley', he went into service with a portly gentleman who was the kindest master that ever could be, but who was, like Mr. Pickwick, vaguely 'retired'. Bob Cratchit's price in the clerk market was 15s. a week, or he would have left Scrooge long before; but when his employer, on conversion, raised his salary and offered to help his family besides, there were the accumulated resources of years of personal miserhood to draw on. When Boffin got his legacy, or thought he had, his job was already over: he had in fact so little direct connexion with the money he spent so generously that in the end it turned out to belong to somebody else. Pa Meagles, it is true, whose employment of Tattycoram should be set against Fagin's employment of Oliver Twist, kept a pair of scales and a money-scoop on his counter-desk even in retirement at Twickenham, as reminders that he had been a banker: but his globe-trotting, his

payment of Henry Gowan's debts, his immunity from
the Merdle crash, mark him as a man whose serious
economic cares were behind him. John Jarndyce, who
had somehow evaded the consequences of the great
suit, must remain a mystery. In all these cases when
Dickens wanted to illustrate a good and generous employer he detached him in one way or another from
the circumstances that made generosity at all difficult.
It is all the more pointed because everybody else's
financial position is so clear.

The one straight example of Christmas-spirit employers, still active in business, earning the means of
kindness in the general racket, are the Cheerybles,
German-merchants. Socialists and commonsense have
agreed to detest them. Bagehot, speaking with
authority about Victorian business-men, said: 'The
Messrs. Cheeryble are among the stupidest of his characters. He forgot that breadth of platitude is rather
different from breadth of sagacity.' Even children have
a horror of their smiles and hand-rubbing seen through
glass, of their placid unremitting unctuousness. But
the horror has another added to it—horror at the utter
dependence of their employees upon them. The whole
Nickleby family falls into their hands and is as firmly
chained to their goodwill as Tim Linkinwater has been
for years. Tim has lost all personality under their
kindness, all desire for change.

> 'Quite right, my dear brother. If he won't listen to
> reason, we must do it against his will, and show him we
> are determined to exert our authority. We must quarrel
> with him, brother Charles.'   [Chapter XXXV.]

Nicholas was promptly set on the same road. He 'was
appointed to the vacant stool in the counting-house
of Cheeryble Brothers, with a present salary of one
hundred and twenty pounds a year' and a furnished
cottage at nominal rent thrown in—which is very much

more than he was worth. A film of hopeless gratitude is spread upon the cash nexus between man and man.

To the Cheerybles we should perhaps add Scrooge's old employer, Fezziwig. For though he appears only for an evening's fun and games and had spent on the whole entertainment 'but a few pounds of your mortal money: three or four perhaps', he poses in that one evening another problem of the time—how can the boss be decently merry with his underlings? Our answer now is: '*Not* in Fezziwig's way.' We even shudder at the depths of bad taste beneath Dickens's praise of him:

> He rubbed his hands; adjusted his capacious waistcoat; laughed all over himself, from his shoes to his organ of benevolence; and called out in a comfortable, oily, rich, fat, jovial voice:
>
> 'Yo ho, there! Ebenezer! Dick!'
>
> [*Christmas Carol*, Stave II.]

The young Scrooge would more likely have sulked in a corner, hot with embarrassment at the Fezziwigs making such fools of themselves, resenting their determined goodness. It is said in sober history that employees sometimes left Robert Owen's model factory at New Lanark because there was too much compulsory music and dancing. And if we look at Helps's *Claims of Labour* (1844)—a book which has been rather obscured by Mill's review of it—we shall find an attempt to guard against this very danger:

> Without interfering too much, or attempting to force a 'Book of Sports' upon the people, who, in that case, would be resolutely dull and lugubrious, the benevolent employer of labour might exert himself in many ways to encourage healthful and instructive amusements amongst his men.

In fiction Dickens let the instruction go rip—Greenwich Fair, Astley's, Sleary's Circus, a dozen oysters and a pot of porter were nearer the mark: but in life he was a ready speaker at Athenaeums, Polytechnics, and Mechanics' Institutions.

We must, I think, conclude that all these attempts to show the working of the Christmas spirit in the relations between master and man are either cheats or failures—at least that they are so on the employers' side. What success they have, in very various degree, is due to the skill we have already noticed with which Dickens has built up the needs and troubles of those to whom even such kindness is a godsend. Those of his characters who are benevolent from above appear now as mere Machines of Fortune. But it is impossible to understand what he was trying to do if we concentrate only on what the Christmas attitude positively set out to teach: it is far more important for what it was meant to counteract. There was, of course, Mammonism in general—the money-greed, go-getting, and vulgar snobbery of the bourgeoisie which Marx praised Dickens for portraying; there was the dim prudery which the middle classes were beginning to use as their mark of social distinction from the lower; jovial open-handedness was consciously set off against these. The peculiarly personal, man-to-man goodness, which gives the Cheerybles or Boffin (all three risen from the working classes) their almost infinite capacity for patronage, can be partly explained as an attempt to keep alive the virtues of domestic industry and business when the old relationships—master, apprentice, journeyman—were going for ever. The element of irresponsibility, almost anarchy, in the Cheerybles can be accounted for partly by their loss of such conventional forms. The law, which has preserved a form of apprenticeship even to the present day, allowed Dickens to praise that kind of relationship: Mr. Witherden the notary is very handsome and benign to Abel Garland on the completion of his articles; flowers are presented and wine is drunk. In the Christmas story *No Thorough-fare*,[1] Walter Wilding has ambitions to restore, in a consciously revivalist spirit, domestic business methods:

> I want a thoroughly good housekeeper to undertake this dwelling-house of Wilding and Co., Wine Merchants, Cripple Corner, so that I may restore in it some of the old relations betwixt employer and employed! So that I may live in it on the spot where my money is made! So that I may daily sit at the head of the table at which the people in my employment eat together, and may eat of the same roast and boiled, and drink of the same beer! So that the people in my employment may lodge under the same roof with me!

'To do my duty to those dependent on me,' he says, 'has a patriarchal and pleasant air about it.' But this neurotic young idealist is a foundling who comes into the business by mysterious ways, and intends his schemes as a recompense for his childhood: 'I, who never knew a father of my own, wish to be a father to all in my employment.' He, too, is thus very far removed from the ordinary circumstances of business life; and in 1867 his creators slightly smiled at him.

As positive contributions to social reform these sketches of good employers betray uneasiness and lack of conviction. The same may be said of much Early Victorian literature on similar lines. *The Claims of Labour*, which falls somewhere between Young England and the Christian Socialists (Helps worked for a time with Maurice and Kingsley in 1848), applies similar ideals to domestic service and the factories. Though Helps is far more aware than Dickens of the dangers of patronizingness, he leaves the impression that ultimately personal benevolence is not enough; at best it seems a palliative.

But the contemporary force and popularity of such books did not derive so much from their positive

---

[1] Wilkie Collins was joint-author with Dickens.

doctrine as from their implied or explicit opposition to the Economists and Philosophical Radicals. Bagehot contrasts with Philosophical Radicalism the 'sentimental' radicalism of Dickens. Bad taste is a tricky, relative thing, and if we now wonder how Fezziwig's 'oily, rich, fat, jovial voice' could have seemed tolerable,[1] even to Dickens, in the 'forties, we must look for the answer in Harriet Martineau and the *Westminster Review*.

In the early days of the *Westminster*, the mid-'twenties, a general opinion of the Philosophical Radicals was formed which later history altered little:

'We found,' wrote Mill in his autobiography, 'all the opinions to which we attached most importance, constantly attacked on the ground of feeling. Utility was denounced as cold calculation; political economy as hard-hearted; anti-population doctrines as repulsive to the natural feelings of mankind. We retorted by the word "sentimentality", which, along with "declamation" and "vague generalities", served us as common terms of opprobrium. Although we were generally in the right, as against those who were opposed to us, the effect was that the cultivation of feeling (except the feelings of public and private duty), was not in much esteem among us, and had little place in the thoughts of most of us, myself in particular. What we principally thought of, was to alter people's opinions; to make them believe according to evidence, and know what was their real interest. . . . While fully recognizing the superior excellence of unselfish benevolence and love of justice, we did not expect the regeneration of mankind from any direct action on those sentiments, but from the effect of educated intellect, enlightening the selfish feelings.'

Mill's account of how he himself outgrew the severe mood of his youth, intensely moving and important as it is in retrospect, records a shifting of opinion which could not be apparent to the public, of which the fruits began to appear only with the publication of his

[1] In *Barchester Towers* (1852) Trollope used 'oily' in disapproval of Mr. Slope.

Political Economy in 1848; and even then the changes appeared in points too technical for the general reader to grasp that a whole spiritual phase in English politics was coming to an end.

General mistrust of its cold spirit, which always prevented any widespread theoretical acceptance of Utilitarianism, prevailed so long as the philosophy itself prevailed; and the Dickens ideal of personal benevolence, contrasted with utilitarian calculation, thus remained topical and popular as long as he was writing. But though from the foundation of the *Westminster* till well into the second half of the century public opinion remained critical or incredulous of the moral theories of the Philosophical Radicals, and though the religious spirit of the time resisted the reduction of ethics to an exact science, neither the incredulity nor the resistance applied in the same way to the theories of the political economists with whom the Philosophical Radicals were associated. Many of the economists' conclusions may have seemed hard-hearted, but as their statistics grew in volume and their arguments in solidity, and as the *Westminster* year by year continued its propaganda in their cause, it became more and more difficult for the ordinary man to doubt the likeness in the gloomy portrait they drew of the world.

Carlyle's phrase, 'the dismal science', has been so often quoted, that there is a risk of thinking that the opinion behind it was confined to him and his followers; but the opinion was widespread, and thought to be a justifiable inference from the works of the economists: 'No one,' said J. E. Cairnes,[1] 'can have studied political economy in the works of its earlier cultivators without being struck with the dreariness of the outlook which, in the main, it discloses for the human race. It seems to have been Ricardo's deliberate opinion that a substantial improvement in the condition of the mass of

[1] In Appendix to Bain's *John Stuart Mill*, 1882.

mankind was impossible.' It is not merely that the Malthusian principle of population and the doctrine that wages must normally and necessarily fall to the minimum point were gladly accepted by wicked exploiters as the justification of their profits; but thousands whose immediate interests were not touched by these beliefs found it difficult to avoid them. Neither the technique of economic argument nor experience of industrial conditions made convincing refutation possible. Sadler, for instance, in his critique of Malthus,[1] won a lot of moral sympathy, but the invention of a new law of population of his own detracted from the effectiveness of his attack upon that of Malthus. The uneasiness of Carlyle's scorn and the rather clown-like exaggerations of Dickens's satire of statisticians and economists are partly to be explained by the underlying doubt whether they might not be right after all. Both were expressing wishes rather than convictions.

Mr. Filer's statistical analysis of tripe, in *The Chimes*, hardly suggests McCulloch:

> Tripe is without an exception the least economical, and the most wasteful article of consumption that the markets of this country can by possibility produce. The loss upon a pound of tripe has been found to be, in the boiling, seven-eighths of a fifth more than the loss upon a pound of any other animal substance whatever. Tripe is more expensive, properly understood, than the hothouse pine-apple. Taking into account the number of animals slaughtered yearly within the bills of mortality alone; and forming a low estimate of the quantity of tripe which the carcases of those animals, reasonably well butchered, would yield; I find that the waste on that amount of tripe, if boiled, would victual a garrison of five hundred men for five months of thirty-one days each, and a February over. The Waste, the Waste!'

Trotty stood aghast, and his legs shook under him. He seemed to have starved a garrison of five hundred men with his own hand.

[1] *The Law of Population*, by Michael Thomas Sadler, 1830.

71

Yet even so, the portrait of Filer had been altered and toned down by Forster. In drawing it, Dickens claimed that he had been directly provoked by the *Westminster Review*. 'Bear in mind,' he wrote to Forster,[1] 'that the *Westminster Review* considered Scrooge's presentation of the turkey to Bob Cratchit as grossly incompatible with political economy.' This seems to have been a joke of his own invention; for the only mention of *A Christmas Carol* in the *Westminster* between its publication and the writing of this letter is a notice to say there is not space to review it. Dickens was joking about objections that had never been made; but it certainly seems likely that Forster objected in the original Filer to exaggeration and crudity which might well have laid Dickens open to accusations of ignorance. For Dickens was clearly not quite happy or confident about *The Chimes*, for all that its ending made him have what women call 'a real good cry'. He consented to have 'the Young England gentleman' knocked out altogether, and at the last minute sketched in his place the man who was always praising the good old times. Even in its final form, the story obviously owes a good deal to Carlyle. When he was planning the famous reading of it to a party of friends after he came back to London from abroad, Dickens twice insisted that Carlyle must be present. The weakness of Mr. Filer is that in him Dickens is trying to satirize something which he cannot show to have disastrous results in practice; Filer as a thinking and speaking machine does not lend himself to Dickens's method; he is too theoretical. For Dickens to satirize a theory he had to be able to show it as hateful or absurd in its effects, as in the 'Third Quarter' he shows the effects of jail upon Fern.

But the importance of the story as a piece of social criticism does not depend on its detailed and direct satire so much as on the contrast of moral moods.

[1] *Life*, Book IV, Chapter 5.

Dickens spoke somewhere of writing 'with a broad grin' and expressing 'the very soul of jollity and happiness'. This was some way removed from the Westminster view of benevolence:

> *Charity*,—in various forms, in one or other of its multiplied disguises,—seems to be the only panacea which occurs to the Great; especially the well-meaning Great of our metropolis. One party advocates a more liberal poor law; another, shorter hours of labour to be enforced by law. In the view of some, *allotments* are the one thing needful; while Young England suggests alms-giving in the magnificent and haughty style of the feudal ages; and Lord Ashley commits his latest solecism, in getting up a society for the protection of Distressed Needlewomen. The same vulgar, shallow, aristocratic error runs through all. Everyone thinks of *relieving*, no one of *removing*, the mischief. The prevailing idea evidently is . . . *to give benefits to an inferior*, not to *do justice to a fellow man*. There is something essentially pauperising in all their conceptions. It pervades alike the factory and mining legislation of Lord Ashley; the 'cricketing' condescension of Lord John Manners, and the insulting rewards and prizes offered by ostentatious landlords to the hampered farmers and the starving peasantry. We are weary of this cuckoo-cry—*always charity, never justice*;—always the *open purse*, never the *equal* measure.
>
> [W. R. Greg, in *Westminster Review*, June 1845.]

Dickens knew that such 'equality' often meant oppression, and that philosophical 'justice' often meant misery: he laughed at Young England as much as Greg sneered. But in trying to re-state Greg's virtue he fell into Lord John Manners's vice.

Dickens had probably read little or nothing of the economists themselves: he had certainly made no serious attempt to understand their theories. But in various forms, according to intelligence and circumstances, the leading ideas of *laissez-faire* and the Malthusian principle of population were current everywhere; and the

73

science of statistics had a fortunate popular symbol in the great calculating-machine of Charles Babbage. It is often said that Dickens, uneducated and a small reader, disliked theory merely because it was theory; it is more important that he disliked particular current theories. To find the right nasty form of them it would be useless to look in John Mill or McCulloch; but Harriet Martineau provides exactly what we want. She was the great intermediary between the theorists and the public, who understood enough to expound but not to doubt her masters' doctrines; and she mercilessly used fiction in her teaching. Her zeal carried her to extremes where few could follow. Her story, *Cousin Marshall*, for instance, condemns not only all poor-relief and voluntary charity, but also the building of labourers' cottages, hospitals, and even almshouses for the aged, as tending to keep up the pauper population. In another story, *Weal and Woe at Garveloch*, a man who is described as a model of prudence and propriety decides that though his means and his intended bride's are quite enough to support a family and keep them from want, still he will not marry her, because from the inconsiderateness of their neighbours the population will increase too rapidly. Much as he loves and approves her he decides to live a single life to check, as far as he can, the tendency of the population to increase in an alarming ratio. Harriet Martineau is therefore just the right person to explain the opposite extremes in Dickens, and her considered opinion of him in the late 'forties has special weight:

It is scarcely conceivable that anyone should, in our age of the world, exert a stronger social influence than Mr. Dickens has in his power. His sympathies are on the side of the suffering and the frail; and this makes him the idol of those who suffer, from whatever cause. We may wish that he had a sounder social philosophy, and that he could suggest a loftier moral to sufferers;—could lead them to see that 'man

74

does not live by bread alone', and that his best happiness
lies in those parts of his nature which are only animated and
exalted by suffering, if it does not proceed too far;—could
show us something of the necessity and blessedness of homely
and incessant self-discipline, and dwell a little less fondly on
the grosser indulgences and commoner beneficence which
are pleasant enough in their own place, but which can never
make a man and society so happy as he desires them to
become.

[*History of the Thirty Years' Peace*, Book VI, Chapter XVI.]

Necessity and Blessedness! In the linking of those
two words is seen the grim alliance between Malthusianism and Nonconformity, against which so much of
Dickens's social benevolence was a protest. Malthus
hung over England like a cloud. It is difficult now to
realize what it meant to thousands of good and sensible
men that they believed his principle of population to
be exactly true—believed that as poverty was relieved
and the standard of life raised, so surely there would
be bred a new race hovering on the misery-line, on the
edge of starvation. However they might wish it false,
they feared it true: they gladly caught for temporary
relief at Carlyle's scorn of such a notion; but when the
shouting died and the effect of loud words wore off,
the ghastly ratios crept back again to haunt them,
attended by the ghastlier checks—vice and misery.
The only ray of hope was in the third check—moral
or prudential restraint. Let the poor live hard lives,
sober, celibate, and unamused; let them eat the plainest
food, pinch to save, and save to lower the rates—then
'civilization' might win through. And how aptly it fitted
the gloomier Christian virtues! Shut the gin-shops,
prevent travelling on the only day a working-man can
travel, make copulation even in marriage seem a sin,
and then there might be seen a heaven on earth according to the Rev. T. R. Malthus, late Professor in the
East India Company's College at Haileybury. 'Homely

and incessant self-discipline' was, for the poor, a necessary consequence of natural law, and blessed by a perversion of the Scriptures. 'You shall have the poor always with you': so it was quoted by Mr. Podsnap.

Seen against this background a great deal in Dickens which might otherwise look merely wayward and sententious, becomes intelligible. The extravagant, exaggerated generosity of the Cheerybles and the converted Scrooge is a counterblast to an exaggerated, extravagant emphasis on Prudence: 'the grosser indulgences' of brandy-drinking, turkey-eating, and circus-going, which his poor people so gladly take to when they can, are meant to put self-discipline upheld by theory in its place. Dickens had no illusions about the good old times; his smoking joints and portly landlords are not bits of Young Englandish revivalism: they are meant to assert that here and now, in 1839 or 1848, 'Malthus Notwithstanding',[1] a lot of good food and good drink is among the best things in life, and for a poor man better still. He had little interest in the food of the rich—people merely played with unnamed luxuries at Merdle's dinner-parties—but Kit Nubbles ordering oysters, Toodle getting his teeth into a slab of bread and butter, or Rumty Wilfer having dinner with 'the beautiful lady' at Greenwich, sends him into ecstasies —and damn the population principle. The careless fertility of his women damns it again. One of his dummy books was called *Malthus's Nursery Songs*.

[1] This was the title of an essay published by W. R. Greg in *Enigmas of Life*, 1872. It was written earlier; but after revision Greg still speaks—when Dickens had been dead two years—of Malthus's doctrine as 'the fixed axiomatic belief of the educated world'. The cloud can only be said to have blown over when it was found the birth-rate was falling.

CHAPTER IV

ECONOMY:
DOMESTIC AND POLITICAL—II

Here's a pair of razors that'll shave you closer than the Board
of Guardians.   DR. MARIGOLD

THE growth of Charitable Institutions in the
Dickens period is admirably shown in the tabu-
lated figures of London Charities in 1862, given by
Sampson Low and reprinted by Mr. E. C. P. Lascelles.[1]
Out of a total of 640 institutions 279 were founded
between 1800 and 1850, and 144 between 1850 and
1860. And other charities, founded since the beginning
of the century, had died before the year to which these
figures apply. A charitable institution may, broadly
speaking, be founded with one of two main aims in
view. It may be to supply services which nothing but
an institution can supply—as hospitals, orphanages,
and schools, which require buildings, a trained staff, and
some assured income before they can do their work at
all; or it may be to provide a channel of benevolence
towards the poor in general, benevolence which might
otherwise be shown to 'undeserving' people who would
throw money away or spend it at the nearest pub. The
distinction between these two objects cannot be rigidly
maintained; but it is useful in considering Dickens's
view of organized charity.

For his attitude, if we take 'organized charity' to be
all of a piece, cannot possibly be called consistent.
Mr. Bernard Darwin in his Introduction to a recent
reprint of Dickens's speeches, praising the bold justice
of his attack on the administration of the Royal Literary
Fund, adds in a parenthesis, 'how he did hate organized

[1] *Early Victorian England*, Volume II, pp. 320–1.

charity!'; but a large proportion of the speeches that follow in the book were delivered with the single object of raising funds for organized charities of one kind or another. He speaks for the Children's Hospital, for the benevolent institutions of Artists, Newsvendors, Railwaymen, Printers' Readers, Gardeners, Warehousemen, and Clerks. His letters to the Press and other active work for Ragged Schools are well known. Yet in the novels and stories organized charity is almost universally condemned with effective acrimony; he rarely attempted to describe the working of an organized charity that he approved: the Children's Hospital in *Our Mutual Friend* is almost the only instance. Very rarely do the beneficent characters 'subscribe' (as distinct from direct personal giving): there is the whispered munificence of Scrooge when he meets the collector again by chance in the street; and there is the Cheerybles' donation to Mr. Trimmers for the man who was smashed, sir, by a cask of sugar. Neither has any prominence in the story. Both were early, while the speeches for good causes become more common in the later years.

One thing is clear—that Dickens hated any charity that had a stigma: Dombey's charity to Rob the Grinder, which made him wear a uniform that brought flocks of jeering boys round his heels, was nearly as bad in Dickens's mind as the kindness of a Board of Guardians. The stigma is not necessarily so tangible as a uniform; it may be the patronizing intrusiveness of Mrs. Pardiggle to the brickmaker, or the complacent condescension of Sir Joseph and Lady Bowley. Such charity is not only unpleasant to the recipients, but bad in its effect on the givers: the moral had been drawn even in *Sketches by Boz*. The *Ladies' Societies* in the *Sketches from Our Parish* shows the peculiar popularity of good works before the name Victorian could be applied to them:

Our Parish is very prolific in ladies' charitable institutions. In winter, when wet feet are common, and colds not scarce, we have the ladies' soup distribution society, the ladies' coal distribution society, and the ladies' blanket distribution society; in summer, when stone fruits flourish and stomach aches prevail, we have the ladies' dispensary, and the ladies' sick visitation committee; and all the year round we have the ladies' child's examination society, the ladies' bible and prayer-book circulation society, and the ladies' childbed-linen monthly loan society. The two latter are decidedly the most important. . . .

The sketch, which is so clearly a preliminary announcement of Mrs. Pardiggle without her Puseyism, is a short history of the rivalry of the distribution society and the child's examination society, and victory is secured for the former by the importation of an orator from Exeter Hall:

. . . the orator (an Irishman) came. He talked of green isles —other shores—vast Atlantic—bosom of the deep—Christian charity—blood and extermination—mercy in hearts—arms in hands—altars and homes—household gods. He wiped his eyes, he blew his nose, and he quoted Latin. The effect was tremendous—the Latin was a decided hit. Nobody knew exactly what it was about, but everybody knew it must be affecting, because even the orator was overcome.

And he was a warning of the future Mr. Honeythunder.

In *Our Mutual Friend* and *Edwin Drood* the hatred of certain kinds of charity is as marked as it had been over thirty years before—there is even a new bitterness in it. Mr. Lascelles, while accepting the view that 'the great increase in charitable subscriptions in the early nineteenth century may have been due in part to fear of revolution', yet goes on to say that if the Victorians 'began to give in fear they went on giving long after fear had given place to complete security; they continued to give when public services were displacing the institutions which their gifts had supported; and they gave no less freely when the possibilities of ostentation and self-glorification were replaced by the modern method, which tends to limit publicity to an entry in the annual report'. But it was in 1865, when security seemed come for ever, that Boffin cried out in the agony of his wealth:

> If there's a good thing to be done, can't it be done on its own merits? If there's a bad thing to be done, can it ever be Patroned and Patronessed right? Yet when a new Institution's going to be built, it seems to me that the bricks and mortar ain't made of half so much consequence as the Patrons and Patronesses; no, nor yet the objects. I wish somebody would tell me whether other countries get Patronized to anything like the extent of this one! And as to the Patrons and Patronesses themselves, I wonder they're not ashamed of themselves. They ain't Pills, or Hair-Washes, or Invigorating Nervous Essences, to be puffed in that way!
> [*Our Mutual Friend*, Book II, Chapter XIV.]

For it was exactly the continuance of the charities into a period of social security that increased their complacency. In the 'thirties and 'forties, though charitable contributions may often have been made in fear, they were at least made with some belief in the pressing urgency of relief and with some knowledge of the appalling poverty which had to be relieved. But by the 'sixties to 'subscribe' to a certain number of charities every year had begun to be a mere matter of routine good form. The father, perhaps, had first subscribed to the Ragged Schools because he was genuinely stirred (not necessarily in his conscience) by the propaganda of Dickens and Lord Ashley; the son might continue the subscription merely because he thought it would look bad to let it drop, or even just because he thought his name would look well with those of dukes and lordlings in the annual report. For fashion does not necessarily demand an ostentatious advertisement of virtue:

Large fat private double letter, sealed with ducal coronet. 'Nicodemus Boffin, Esquire. My dear Sir—Having consented to preside at the forthcoming Annual Dinner of the Family Party Fund, and feeling deeply impressed with the immense usefulness of that noble Institution and the great importance of its being supported by a List of Stewards that shall prove to the public the interest taken in it by popular and distinguished men, I have undertaken to ask you to become a Steward on that occasion. Soliciting your favourable reply before the 14th instant, I am, My Dear Sir, Your faithful servant, LINSEED. P.S. The Steward's fee is limited to three Guineas.' Friendly this, on the part of the Duke of Linseed (and thoughtful in the postscript), only lithographed by the hundred and presenting but a pale individuality of address to Nicodemus Boffin, Esquire, in quite another hand.   [Book I, Chapter XVII.]

Such blatant use of snobbery in appeals for charity (it persists to-day) was an obvious target for Dickens's jokes; but the snob-appeal was itself a product of mid-Victorian conditions. The Mendicity Society founded in 1818 was one of the first institutions to publish an annual report with lists of subscribers; but among the subscribers in the bad winter of 1838, for instance, very few titled people appear, and the Society was still looked on with some suspicion by the magistrates and police as meddlesome and slightly subversive. Yet this Society was in many ways the father of the Victorian system: it was among the first to issue tickets to subscribers which could be given to beggars in place of money and then changed for food or lodging at the Society's offices. This practice underlined the important distinction between the 'deserving' and the 'undeserving' poor which is implicit in Dickens's treatment of this whole subject. His work—especially his journalism—is full of exposures of the professional begging-letter writers and all the charlatan traders upon compassion who haunted the streets of London;

but the false poor can gain only when the true poor are known to exist; it is they who parody society's short-comings with their hired babies and acquired sores. A conversation was overheard between two mothers who had rented babies for the day:

> 'How much did you give for yours?'
> 'A shilling a-piece.'
> 'A shilling a-piece!—Vy then you've been done, or babbies is riz; one or t'other—I only give sixpence for mine, and they feeds 'em and Godfrey's-cordials 'em and all, afore I takes 'em, into the bargain.'
>
> [*Quarterly Review*, Vol. 64, p. 355.]

—a dialogue that Dickens himself might have seemed bold to use. The exploiters behind these women were extreme examples of a kind he detested.

When he was attacking the begging-letter writers he insisted that the genuine poor do not use such methods:

> The poor never write these letters. Nothing could be more unlike their habits. The writers are public robbers; and we who support them are parties to their depredations. . . . Let us give all we can; let us give more than'ever. Let us do all we can; let us do more than ever. But let us give, and do, with a high purpose; not to endow the scum of the earth, to its own greater corruption, with the offals of our duty.   [*Household Words*, May 18, 1850.]

But ticket-charity was the most obvious method of distinguishing between these 'public robbers' and the genuine poor. Even in the 'thirties such various institutions as the Lying-in Hospital, the Welsh Dispensary, the City Dispensary, the London Dispensary, the Institution for the Diseases of Children, the Rupture Society, the Ophthalmic Infirmary, the City of London Truss Society, the Blanket Society, the Spitalfields Association for the Distribution of Coals, Bread, and

Potatoes were among those which worked on the ticket-system.[1] It is not accidental that this system found greater favour as Malthusian doctrines spread. The great growth in the number and scope of organized charities in the period does not indicate only an increase in goodwill (this cannot be estimated), but also an increase of caution in the exercise of it. If money was subscribed to a recognized institution with such safeguards, the giver knew, or thought he knew, that it would be prudently laid out and handed on only to the deserving, and only for necessities. Indiscriminate almsgiving was considered almost as great a fault as the giving of nothing at all: it tended to encourage dependence, pauperism, and unthrift, the great Malthusian vices.

Smiles's *Self-Help*, the great text-book of mid-Victorian casuistry, is chiefly designed to teach the corresponding virtues of prudence and thrift. See, for instance, the chapter called 'Money—its Use and Abuse':

> The man who is always hovering on the verge of want is in a state not far removed from that of slavery. He is in no sense his own master, but is in constant peril of falling under the bondage of others, and accepting the terms which they dictate to him. He cannot help being, in a measure, servile, for he dares not look the world boldly in the face; and in adverse times he must look either to alms or the poor's rates. If work fails him altogether, he has not the means of moving to another field of employment; he is fixed to his parish like a limpet to its rock, and can neither migrate nor emigrate.
>
> To secure independence, the practice of simple economy is all that is necessary. Economy requires neither superior courage nor eminent virtue; it is satisfied with ordinary energy, and the capacity of average minds.[2]   [1866 edn.]

This modified Malthusianism explains a great deal of what often seems so cautious, stingy, and self-righteous

[1] *Extracts from Information . . . Poor Laws*, 1833, p. 290. From Chadwick's report on London.
[2] Compare with this Dr. Arnold's letter of January 20th, 1839, quoted on p. 93.

in Victorian good-works. And as the prudent and thrifty poor tended to be identified with the 'deserving', charity was likely to be restricted to those who scarcely needed it, or to the victims of mere deception and accident. On one hand was the danger of giving to those who did not need, on the other the danger of giving to those who did not deserve: the way between was narrow, but it was the way that Dickens tried to take.

If we judge Mr. Micawber by his behaviour throughout the greater part of *David Copperfield*, there could be no more wanton violator of the rules of Malthus and Smiles. He is the personification of unthrift; he goes on begetting children for whom he cannot provide; he refuses to toe the misery-line; he accepts charitable loans that he cannot possibly hope to repay; he finally has to emigrate on somebody else's money: yet Dickens loves him beyond words. So far he seems a direct, unqualified affront to the whole little prudent philosophy. But all along, secreted within him, there has been an efficient colonial magistrate. That ending of Micawber has often been smiled at as unlikely, derided as bad art, or explained away in general terms as just another instance of Dickens's sentimental liking for a happy finish. Chesterton quoted it as the leading example of that *vulgar* optimism into which Dickens was sometimes betrayed:

> There are cases at the end of his stories in which his kindness to his characters is a careless and insolent kindness. He loses his real charity and adopts the charity of the Charity Organization Society; the charity that is not kind, the charity that is puffed up, and that does behave itself unseemly. At the end of some of his stories he deals out his characters a kind of out-door relief.   [*Charles Dickens*, Chapter XI.]

But vulgar though this may be, Dickens did it with his eyes fully open. He never meant Micawber to be a Chestertonian saint who 'never ought to succeed', whose 'kingdom is not of this world'. He thought of his plots in worldly terms, and Micawber was a very practical optimist when he contemplated the Medway Coal Trade. The moral of Micawber rather is that even in a man as fantastically improvident and as gay about it as he, there is a secret possibility of success. This moral is plainly more trite than Chesterton's; but its triteness was peculiarly topical. For Micawber got the better of the prudent philosophers both on the swings and on the roundabouts. For sixty-two chapters he was saying in the very best Dickens manner, 'See how wonderful and lovable a thoroughly unthrifty and imprudent man can be,' and in the sixty-third he turned round and showed that even he could do well enough for himself when the right thing turned up. Vulgarity loses more than half its grossness by being seen in the context.

For Dickens ultimately accepted the distinction between the deserving and the undeserving poor, and in that he was a man of his time. The undeserving poor in his novels, like Good Mrs. Brown in *Dombey and Son* or Rogue Riderhood and Mr. Dolls in *Our Mutual Friend*, are as bad as irremediable vice can make them. But he used the distinction as a peg on which to hang his often-repeated sermon that far more of the poor are deserving than the richer are inclined to think; that misfortune, accident, and deception fall more widely than is generally supposed; that the ties which 'link the poor man to his humble hearth are of the true metal and bear the stamp of Heaven'. Very few indeed of his poor people are made out to be undeserving; but when the verdict comes it comes like a thunderbolt and there is no gainsaying. This is vulgar too, and the overwrought hyperbole is partly accounted for by the uneasy consciousness that Charles Dickens, Apostle of the People, was marching with his enemies, and could not quite see the way out. Also, of course, he loved a good crime and there had to be somebody to commit it. None of his undeserving poor are bad because they are lazy: they are all abundantly active in their wickedness, working as hard as the good. There is no example of the merely unthrifty, careless, ignorant, but not evil person whom Malthus took to be the backbone of the working-class.

Ticket-charity has the great disadvantage of being too suspicious: it implies that the many are undeserving and the few are not. It hurts the pride of the honest recipient (like the new Poor Law) and absolves the giver from all personal knowledge of those to whom he gives: its methods are too cold; it subverts the Dickens ideal of man-to-man goodness. There is nowhere in the novels a charitable organization that deals in general almsgiving on the subscription and ticket method. The one set description of a good organized charity is of an institution doing work which could not be satisfactorily done by individual private benevolence. The Children's Hospital described at the end of Chapter IX of *Our Mutual Friend* would have been unhesitatingly identified with the Great Ormond Street Hospital for which Dickens had made such an excellent speech at the Anniversary Dinner of 1858. The fiction, an attempt to recapture earlier brilliance, is not so good as the speech; yet it was a piece of plain propaganda for a specific object,[1] and the death-bed of Johnny is worth the death-beds of Nell and Paul and Jo all put together.

The extreme case of the offensive busybody charity satirized in the *Sketches*, in Mrs. Pardiggle, and in the people who pestered Boffin, is to be found in Mrs. Jellyby: but in her another point of criticism is added to the obvious neglect of her children for 'the cause'—a point which shows Dickens once more in close connexion

---

[1] Dickens's views about the proper management of hospitals veered unsystematically between admiration for 'Supported entirely by Voluntary Contributions' and for a state system such as he had seen working in America.

with Carlyle. He was as fierce as Carlyle against the kind of philanthropy which bothered with negroes and overseas barbarians while barbarism flourished and spread at home. Mrs. Jellyby hoped 'to have from a hundred and fifty to two hundred healthy families cultivating coffee and educating the natives of Borrioboola-Gha, on the left bank of the Niger'. Ten years before *Bleak House* came out—that is about the time that Esther first went to the Jellyby house—the African Civilization Society and Niger Association, largely managed by Fowell Buxton, got up a hare-brained expedition which most readers would have taken to be Dickens's model. 'We read in the chronicles of the time,' says Miss Martineau, 'of public meetings, with Prince Albert in the Chair, so crowded that persons were carried out fainting; of the gratulations and mutual praises of statesmen and prelates, of grand subscriptions and yet grander hopes.' An expedition of three iron steamers, two of which were appropriately named the *Albert* and the *Wilberforce*, was prepared in the Thames, and, after a visit from the Prince Consort, sailed bravely for Africa. There were scientists on board and two representatives of the C.M.S. The purpose was double—to open up trade on the upper Niger, and to establish a model farm there as a centre of beneficent Christian civilization. Numbers died of malignant fever, and the whole attempt was abandoned within a year. Buxton's main aim had been to deflect Africans from the slave-trade by the alternative of 'legitimate' commerce. The Borrioboola-Gha venture failed because of the 'King of Borrioboola wanting to sell everybody—who survived the climate—for rum'.

The Jellyby episode in *Bleak House* is an excellent example of the strength and the weakness of Dickens's use of fiction as a medium of social criticism: it is prodigiously strong in personalities, but weak in arguments. The inference is that because Mrs. Jellyby is ridiculous, everything she advocates is automatically ridiculous. The conclusion is given in one of the better pieces of Richard's sense, that 'her eyes had a curious habit of seeming to look a long way off, as if they could see nothing nearer than Africa'. One may well agree that the personal-dramatic method is the proper method of fiction, and that a novel cannot be killed more thoroughly than by debate. But the episode has other shortcomings; for the personal drama of the Borrioboola-Gha venture took place, not in Mrs. Jellyby's first-floor front, but on the left bank of the Niger. Dickens himself realized this; for he had published in 1848[1] an article on the Niger Expedition which is remarkable even to-day for its vigour, eloquence, and even, in places, enlightenment. He has quoted from the book he is reviewing an account of the meeting between King Obi and the Commissioners sent by Her Majesty to treat with him. The ending of the slave-trade has been discussed, and the commercial rights, and the purchase of land, and the Christian religion. Less has been said about the blockade and the establishment of forts. This is how Dickens recapitulates the whole pathetic interview:

> Obi, sitting on the quarter-deck of the Albert, looking slyly out from under his savage forehead and his conical cap, sees before him her Majesty's white Commissioners from the distant blockade-country gravely propounding, at one sitting, a change in the character of his people (formed, essentially, in the inscrutable wisdom of God, by the soil they work on and the air they breathe)—the substitution of a religion it is utterly impossible he can appreciate or understand, be the mutual interpretation never so exact and never so miraculously free from confusion, for that in which he has been bred, and with which his priest and jugglers subdue his subjects, the entire subversion of his whole barbarous system of trade and revenue—and the uprooting, in a word,

[1] Reprinted by F. G. Kitton in *To Be Read at Dusk*, etc., 1898, pp. 51 ff.

of all his, and his nation's, preconceived ideas, methods, and customs. In return for this, the white men are to trade with him by means of ships that are to come there one day or other; and are to quell infractions of the treaty by means of other white men, who are to learn how to draw the breath of life there, by some strong charm they certainly have not discovered yet. Can it be supposed that on this earth there lives a man who better knows than Obi, leering round upon the river's banks, the dull dead mangrove trees, the slimy and decaying earth, the rotting vegetation, that these are shadowy promises and shadowy threats, which he may give to the hot winds? . . . 'Too much palaver,' says Obi, with good reason. 'Give me the presents and let me go home, and beat my tom-toms all night long, for joy!'

Sound argument and dramatic effect are there combined, far beyond the Jellyby range, combined, too, with a streak of Carlyle-like contempt. Later he comes back to the exhortation:

The stone that is dropped into the ocean of ignorance at Exeter Hall, must make its widening circles, one beyond another, until they reach the negro's country in their natural expansion. There is a broad, dark sea between the Strand in London, and the Niger, where those rings are not yet shining; and through all that space they must appear, before the last one breaks upon the shore of Africa. Gently and imperceptibly the widening circle of enlightenment must stretch and stretch, from man to man, from people on to people, until there is a girdle round the earth; but no convulsive effort, or far-off aim, can make the last great outer circle first, and then come home at leisure to trace out the inner one. Believe it, African Civilisation, Church of England Missionary, and all other Missionary Societies! The work at home must be completed thoroughly, or there is no hope abroad. To your tents, O Israel! but see they are your own tents!

Bleak House, in passing, enforces the same moral; and to a correspondent who had complained of 'the attack that is conveyed in the sentence about Jo seated in his anguish on the doorstep of the Society for the Propagation of the Gospel in Foreign Parts' [*Bleak House*, Chapter XVI], Dickens wrote:

> There was a long time during which benevolent societies were spending immense sums on missions abroad, when there was no such thing as a ragged school in England, or any kind of associated endeavour to penetrate to those horrible domestic depths in which such schools are now to be found, and where they were, to my most certain knowledge, neither placed nor discovered by the Society for the Propagation of the Gospel in Foreign Parts.
>
> If you think the balance between the home mission and the foreign mission justly held in the present time, I do not.
>
> [Letter of July 9, 1852.]

The increasing interest in Foreign Missions and in pretended philanthropic schemes for the benefit of 'backward' peoples was a phase of British Imperialism of which the implications were not fully seen until after Dickens's death. But already the great technical superiority of Western civilization was creating the assumption of a general cultural and moral superiority which could be used as a justification of expanding Empire. In particular those forms of Christianity which preached salvation by faith rather than by works (Dickens opposed them wherever they appeared) could claim to rescue from eternal damnation the heathen who in his blindness bowed down to wood and stone, without considering either his interests or his utterly different cultural tradition. Dickens's scorn of the idea that formal assent to the phrases of the creeds—the product of an alien scheme of thought and life—could bring about the one essential change in such a man as Obi had the same origin as his hatred of Stiggins, Chadband, and the Murdstones: the hypocrisy was obviously intensified by the gunboats and trade treaties.

He also saw that it was impossible to supplant one culture and civilization, however primitive, by another in a single generation, and that climate and other factors outside human control might altogether distort much that such a change would involve even if it were brought about by a long, patient process of intelligent teaching. Yet in the last resort he did not doubt that the best of British civilization as he understood it was immeasurably better than that of the coloured peoples, and he let himself run with the herd in describing them: Major Bagstock's Indian servant is constructed of mere conventional prejudice. This acceptance of the popular attitude is consistent with the doctrine of *Bleak House*: for if Orientals and Africans are generally inferior to Englishmen, and not potential equals or superiors, it is easier to make it appear a crime that their welfare should be considered while that of so many Englishmen is neglected: education should begin with those thought best likely to benefit by it. The temptation for philanthropic mid-Victorians was to choose the remoter rather than the nearer object for their work because the consequences would affect them less closely, and to assume a superiority that was not secure; to counter this evil Dickens was pushed further than he need have been into a merely negative attitude towards the societies and organizations which were trying in various ways to control the chaos and bitterness in the clash of civilizations.

He had no one consistent attitude to 'Organized Charity'. His dislike of many charities was part of his destructive Benthamism: when he began to write, the Charity Inquiry Commission was discovering in the administration of the older charities abuses as awful and as comic as those unearthed by the Commission on Municipal Corporations. Funds silently appropriated by officers; funds spent on little else but enormous annual dinners; funds wastefully and inefficiently used;

bounties which encouraged hypocrisy and extravagance; endowments so restricted that their purpose
could no longer be fulfilled; inquiry revealed such things
everywhere. The effects of such abuses are shown, for
instance, in the wretched and useless education of Noah
Claypole and Rob the Grinder, and Dickens played his
part in the Benthamite clean-up of the older endowments; but if he had had all his way Christ's Hospital
would no longer be the Blue-Coat School. [See Note A,
p. 105.]

But the desire to reform the charities brought with
it two things that Dickens resisted with all his might—
the Malthusian attempts to limit charity of every kind,
and the new spirit of fussy priggishness and patronage
distilled by the sects and parties of the new benevolence.
The way between these two evils was difficult to steer,
and in trying to take it Dickens betrayed the alter-
nating hesitancy and exaggeration· so common to good
men of his class and time.

But· in one of his great moral campaigns he never
hesitated for an instant; and if the question were
asked in what single respect his benevolent reformism
appeared most consistent and convincing the plainest
answer would be, in his treatment of the Poor Law.
We now read for other reasons the novels in which it
is chiefly discussed. Some adjustment of attention is
needed to see the frighteningly evil world of the later
part of *Oliver Twist*, which has the private emotional
quality of a bad dream, as a proper development of
the opening chapters. We tend rather to think of the
first part as a detached tract, preliminary to the novel
that matters. But for its earliest readers the emotional
connexion would have seemed far closer. The New
Poor Law, which was looked on as the great triumph
of Malthusianism in practice, was introduced in 1834;
Oliver Twist was begun in 1837.

The movement of educated opinion about the new

law in those three years can be excellently followed in
the letters of Dr. Arnold of Rugby. On December 31,
1834, the year in which the law was introduced, he
wrote:

> . . . It delights me to find that so good a man as Mr. H. thinks
> very well of the New Poor Law, and anticipates very favour-
> able results from it, but I cannot think that this or any other
> single measure can do much towards the cure of evils so
> complicated.

Two years later—November 28, 1836—he wrote of

> the Poor Law Act,—a measure in itself wise and just, but
> which, standing alone, and unaccompanied by others of a
> milder and more positively improving tendency, wears an
> air of harshness, and will, I fear, embitter the feelings of the
> poorer classes still more.

Then three years later still he finds his prophecy
fulfilled—January 20, 1839:

> I am inclined to think, that the Poor Law, though I quite
> believe it to be in itself just in its principle, has yet done more
> moral harm, by exasperating the minds of the poor, than it
> can possibly have done good. I am very far, however, from
> wishing to return to the old system; but I think that the
> Poor Law should be accompanied by an organized system
> of Church charity, and also by some acts designed in title,
> as well as in substance, for the relief of the poor, and that
> by other means than driving them into economy by terror.
> Economy itself is a virtue which appears to me to imply an
> existing previous competence; it can surely have no place
> in the most extreme poverty; and for those who have a
> competence to require it of those who have not, seems to me
> to be something very like mockery.

That is a letter in the contemporary Dickens spirit.[1]
There is no need to trace again here the growth of

---

[1] When Forster sent some extracts from the *Life of Arnold* in which these letters
appeared, Dickens replied: 'I respect and reverence his memory beyond all expression. I must have that book. Every sentence that you quote from it is the
text-book of my faith.'

hatred for the Poor Law among the working classes. It is enough to say that the extremely severe winter of 1837–8, the high price of corn, trade depression, and unemployment then made the law even more unpopular than it had been before. A novel could hardly have been more topical than *Oliver Twist*: the season made it so. When in March 1838 a petition was presented to the House of Lords from the Guardians of the Dudley Union, complaining that the diet prescribed by the Commissioners was not adequate to the support of the paupers, England was already laughing over Oliver who 'asked for more'. Dickens's 'three meals of thin gruel a day, with an onion twice a week, and half a roll on Sundays' was, of course, an exaggeration. But the No. 1. Dietary approved and published by the Poor Law Commissioners in 1836 included $1\frac{1}{2}$ pints of gruel for every one of the seven days, and the total food for able-bodied men in the week was as follows:

On three days: 12 ozs. bread; $1\frac{1}{2}$ pints gruel; 5 ozs. cooked meat; $\frac{1}{2}$ lb. potatoes; $1\frac{1}{2}$ pints broth.

On three other days: 12 ozs. bread; $1\frac{1}{2}$ pints gruel; $1\frac{1}{2}$ pints soup; 2 ozs. cheese.

On Fridays: 12 ozs. bread; $1\frac{1}{2}$ pints gruel; 14 ozs. suet or rice pudding; 2 ozs. cheese.[1]

This was divided into three meals a day; women got slightly less, children over nine the same as women; children under nine were to be dieted 'at discretion'. It is fairly plain which way discretion would veer. The Dudley dietary against which the petition was presented was a good deal more generous than this, and did at least include some provision for green vegetables; but there too were the inevitable $1\frac{1}{2}$ pints of gruel a day.

According to the internal chronology *Oliver Twist*

[1] *Second Annual Report of the Poor Law Commissioners* (1836), p. 56. Other slightly better dietaries were also approved. The Dudley diet-table is in *The Annual Register*, 1838, 'History,' pp. 198–9.

must have been born in a workhouse of the old Poor Law. Under Gilbert's Act or one of the numerous local acts such a workhouse as that described in the first chapter was perfectly possible; there were in certain districts, under Gilbert's Act, unions of parishes to maintain them. There were also pauper baby-farms. The new Law must have come in while Oliver was out at grass. When he came back nine years old Bumble was still Beadle; that too was possible: all the details did not change at a stroke, and the early reports of the Commissioners are full of complaints of unsuitable officers taken over from the old system. The new elements in Chapter II are the pure Malthusian policy to which 'the Board' had been converted in Oliver's absence and the systematically low dietary of the 'general mixed' workhouse, by which the aged and infirm, infants and insane suffered for the moral benefit of the able-bodied whom the Poor Law was intended to deter. 'The relief was inseparable from the gruel; and that frightened people.'

The famous 'workhouse-test' was intended primarily as a deterrent. Leaving aside the doctrinaire Malthusianism by which many of its promoters were influenced, the main practical aims of the new Poor Law were to reduce the cost of relief by joining parishes in unions and applying a uniform standard throughout the country; to put an end to the system of supplementing wages out of the poor-rates which was artificially lowering wages and also depriving labourers of self-respecting motives for industry; to take the administration of the law out of the hands of the Justices, who had frequently used it for their own ends; to regularize the conduct of workhouses, which were often squalid, disorderly, miserable, and managed by mercenary sharks. With these aims no unprejudiced person who knew the facts could possibly quarrel. Dickens never mentions them, nor does he discuss the wisdom of the general policy of restricting, as far as possible, outdoor relief for the able-bodied: he concentrates mainly on the bad workhouse feeding, the absurdity of such officers as Bumble and the utter failure to make any proper provision for the pauper children. With these points in mind we can look at Harriet Martineau's criticism of him.

She was, of course, holding a brief for the Commissioners when she called the New Law 'a reform which has saved the state'; but she spoke within the truth when she said that 'the measure was working, all the while, for the extinction of the law-made vices and miseries of the old system'. When she adds, however, that 'the faults of the old law were represented (as by Mr. Dickens in *Oliver Twist*) as those of the new',[1] she becomes a misleading partisan. Whatever may have been true in some isolated parishes nobody would have maintained that underfeeding was a *typical* fault of the old system; bad, wasteful, and dirty feeding there often was, but the common objection was that a pauper, whether in the workhouse or out, often fed better than the man who was getting no relief from the rates. It was the deliberate aim of the reformers to make the diet sparse. Where the Guardians interpreted the official instructions liberally, or where the Workhouse Master was a particularly good manager it was just possible to make do: but the general complaint from all parts of the country, of which the Dudley petition was an extreme example, was that the dietary was inadequate. Dickens exaggerated, as we have seen; but he exaggerated a typical fault of the new law, not of the old.

Miss Martineau's criticism has more force if we take it as applying to the portrait of Bumble: he was, in fact, according to Dickens's own chronology, a relic of the earlier system. But, on the most important point

---

[1] *Autobiography*, I, p. 225.

of all, Dickens's attack was perfectly justified, though he was very bold to make it as early as he did, when the reformers had had only three years to put their plans into practice. For the position of children was bad both under the old law and under the new. The evidence for the old law is excellently given by a writer who had toured East Kent with one of the Assistant Poor Law Commissioners in 1834, just after the reform came in:

> With respect to the manner in which children have been systematically demoralized in many of our small poorhouses, the error, we conceive, speaks so clearly for itself, that we need not offer to be its advocate. A mixture, in about equal parts, (never mind a scruple or two), of boys and girls, idle men, and abandoned women, can only by a miracle be unproductive of evil to society; we will, therefore, content ourselves with repeating a practical opinion which was thus expressed to us by a governor of twenty years' experience:—
> '*When children*,' said Mr. Cadell, '*have been brought up in a work'us, they have never no disposition to shun a work'us.*'
>
> [*Quarterly Review*, April 1835, Vol. 53, p. 481.]

The Commissioners of 1834 had realized that any sound Poor Law must make fundamental distinctions between the various classes of paupers; that the able-bodied unemployed, men and women, the infants, the aged and the infirm cannot all be treated alike, and cannot properly be dealt with all in one institution. They made this distinction in theory and in planning their policy, but they failed to carry it out in practice. The sections of the Webbs' great book which analyse and account for this failure are among the most disturbing records in modern English history. It was partly caused by disagreements among the Commissioners and difficulties in the secretariat, partly by local objections from the parishes. In spite of all that was said and hoped for, the workhouse tended to revert to the 'general mixed' institution which had been such a scandal in the days of Crabbe and Speenhamland. The children suffered most: bad education or none, a stigmatizing uniform, association in the house with vagrant thieves and prostitutes and lunatics, followed by an early 'apprenticeship' (possibly as a climbing boy) without 'after-care', to get him off the rates, made the later progress of a parish boy almost inevitable. Few brought Oliver's priggish innocence from the house or turned out to have for parents a gentleman and the daughter of a naval officer.

It would be extremely interesting to know how far, when Dickens wrote his book, he realized the crucial justice of its first few chapters as a criticism of administrative methods: he was almost prophetic. The question is whether the workhouse to which Oliver was taken back after leaving Mrs. Mann's was the identical building in which he had been born, or whether the 'large stone hall' in which the boys were fed was part of one of the new Bastilles set up according to the Commissioners' plans.[1] If it was the old building, Dickens was writing about faults of the old law allowed to continue under the new; and his work would be propaganda for the recommendations of the original Commissioners; if it was one of the new buildings, it was propaganda against the rejuvenation of abuses in a more unpleasant form, a direct attack on administrative failure which would come home more keenly after grand but broken promises. In either case Harriet Martineau, writing her *Autobiography* in the 'fifties, might have seen that even then the problems of educating and training pauper children were hardly tackled, if she had not been partly blinded by her fixed opinions of years before. For by then it was apparent that the

[1] Professor J. H. Clapham (*Early Victorian England*, I, p. 11) assumes that the workhouse was one of the old ones, unaltered between Chapter I and Chapter II. This is rather borne out by the original illustration to the 'asks for more' scene; but the pictures often do not correspond closely to what Dickens himself had in mind.

general mixed workhouse was the standard rather than the exception, and that it was scandalous.

The state of affairs described in these chapters of *Oliver Twist* continued substantially unaltered for many years after the book was published, though the authorities were never immune from criticism and made ineffectual attempts to meet it. The Poor Law Amendment Act of 1843 (7 & 8 Vict. c. 101), provided in Section 34:

> It shall be lawful for the said commissioners, as and when they may see fit, by order under their hands and seal, to declare so many parishes or unions, as they may see fit, to be combined into school districts, for the management of any class or classes of infant poor, not above the age of *sixteen* years, being chargeable to any such parish or union, who are orphans, or are deserted by their parents, or whose parents or surviving parent or guardians are consenting thereto. . . .

This would have provided for cases like Oliver's if only the Act had not contained certain restrictions which put great difficulties in the way of the Commissioners, and made it possible for further objections to be raised by the Parish authorities. In consequence a further Act was required in 1848—'An Act to amend the Law for the Formation of Districts for the Education of Infant Poor', 11 & 12 Vict. c. 82. Under this Act three important school districts were formed in London and an existing school at Norwood was taken over and enlarged by the Poor Law Board. Altogether provision was made for about 2,000 London pauper children. In 1850 Dickens published in the first volume of *Household Words* a laudatory article[1] on this school at Norwood, and another on a similar school at Swinton near Manchester:

'Ought the misdeeds of the parents', asks the latter article,

[1] Not written by himself.

'to be visited on their innocent children? should pauper and outcast infants be neglected so as to become pests to Society, or shall they be so trained as to escape the pauper-spirit, and make amends to Society for the bad citizenship of their parents, by their own persevering industry, economy, and prudence in mature life? Common sense asks, does the State desire good citizens or bad?'

In this way Dickens used his editorship to jog the slow processes of administrative muddle and neglect. Even the burst of activity over pauper children in 1849–50 was largely prompted by fear and shame. For in 1848 Drouet's vast baby-farm at Tooting, where 1,400 children were kept together with awful overcrowding, had an outbreak of cholera in which many children died; and the details revealed at the inquests once more brought the Poor Law authorities unwelcome fame.

Dickens himself wrote for the *Examiner* two articles on the Tooting baby-farm which form the proper historical appendix to *Oliver Twist*. 'The cholera,' he said, 'or some unusually malignant form of typhus assimilating itself to that disease, broke out in Mr. Drouet's farm for children, because it was brutally conducted, vilely kept, preposterously inspected, dishonestly defended, a disgrace to a Christian community, and a stain upon a civilized land.' Apart from Drouet himself, who was ultimately tried for manslaughter, the blames attached to the various London Boards of Guardians who sent their children to the place, and to the central Poor Law authority which allowed it to continue. Dickens makes brisk and damning work of such men as Mr. W. R. James and Mr. Winch who visited Tooting as the representatives of the Holborn Guardians; he trounces the St. Pancras Guardians for culpable carelessness—and so on; he is equally effective against the Poor Law Inspector; but he is less certain of his ground against the Commissioners themselves, where his strongest case lay. 'The Poor Law Commissioners,' he says, 'if they had the power to issue positive orders for its better management (a point which is, however, in question), were as culpable as any of the rest.'

Such caution is quite foreign to the mood of *Oliver Twist*: for if they had not the power, they should have had it. In fact, it seems that they had, but failed to use it. The position was put as follows by *The Justice of the Peace* on January 27, 1849:

It may be, that owing to inattention to the subject, the poor-law boards have not hitherto made regulations which will directly bind the parties who keep these farming establishments for pauper children; and therefore, for the time being, the board may be powerless; or, as Lord *Ebrington* says, 'there would *practically* be much difficulty in enforcing any such control, and in subjecting the establishment in question to the regulations of the board'. But how comes it, we would ask, that the poor-law board is powerless in such a case? Mr. Drouet's establishment, and the others about London, if we rightly understand the matter, are regulated by the provisions of the 7 Geo. 3, c. 39, intituled, 'an Act for the better regulation of parish poor children, of the several parishes therein mentioned, within the bills of mortality'. Now the 15th section of 4 & 5 Will. 4, c. 76, enables the commissioners 'from time to time as they shall see occasion, to make and issue all such rules orders and regulations for the management of the poor, for the government of workhouses, and the education of the children therein, and for the management of parish poor children under the provisions of the 7 Geo. 3, c. 39, *and the superintending, inspecting and regulating of the houses wherein such poor children* are kept and maintained', etc. Surely this will give them power to issue rules, orders, and regulations for the management of such an establishment as that at Tooting. If, then, they have such powers, how comes it, we would ask, that they have not been exercised?

101

In this instance it seems as if Dickens spared the Poor Law Board unnecessarily and allowed himself to be humbugged for once by the evasive language of the Barnacles. But, apart from the technical question of powers, he underlined, after the Drouet case, two of the main doctrines of *Oliver Twist*—that the farming-system led to every kind of cruel abuse and that pauper children, above all others, should not have to suffer a primitive discipline because of circumstances over which they had no control whatever.

The great defect of the Poor Law of 1834 was that it put the screw on all paupers alike, and 'the house' first became the horrible reproach among the poor it remains even to this day. The prodigious patronage of Mr. Dorrit while a prisoner in the Marshalsea towards Old Nandy who 'had retired of his own accord to the Workhouse' and had there become one 'in a grove of two score and nineteen more old men, every one of whom smells of all the others', shows the social depths to which Malthusian orthodoxy had dug:

> Mr. Dorrit was in the habit of receiving this old man as if the old man held of him in vassalage under some feudal tenure. He made little treats and teas for him, as if he came in with his homage from some outlying district where the tenantry were in a primitive state. It seemed as if there were moments when he could by no means have sworn but that the old man was an ancient retainer of his, who had been meritoriously faithful. When he mentioned him, he spoke of him casually as his old pensioner. He had a wonderful satisfaction in seeing him, and in commenting on his decayed condition after he was gone. It appeared to him amazing that he could hold up his head at all, poor creature. 'In the Workhouse, sir, the Union; no privacy, no visitors, no station, no respect, no speciality. Most deplorable!'   [*Little Dorrit*, Book I, Chapter XXXI.]

But the wonderful old jail-bird was led into an-achronism by his creator; for the tone and language about the workhouse belong to 1856, though he spoke thirty years before.[1]

Betty Higden in *Our Mutual Friend*, wandering over the country with her burial money sewn into her clothes, living with the single aim of keeping off the parish, stands for millions who since 1834 have lived for little else. Most modern readers are bored by her and dislike her for her monotonous talk and apparently stupid wanderings. But, rather surprisingly, Swinburne found her one of Dickens's great characters:

> . . . the martyrdom of Betty Higden—the most nearly intolerable tragedy in all the tragic work of Dickens. Even the unsurpassed and unsurpassable grandeur and beauty of the martyred old heroine's character can hardly make the wonderful record of her heroic agony endurable by those who have been so tenderly and so powerfully compelled to love and to revere her.   [*Charles Dickens*, 1913, p. 61.]

It is hard, perhaps, to see any genuine tragedy in Betty Higden; but what may seem to some the tedious pigheadedness with which she refuses all Boffin's offers of help can be regarded as a gallant dying gesture of independence; her very stupidity is the reverse of many virtues the English Poor Law was destroying. Any one of us in her place would have accepted Boffin's offers. Dickens possibly meant her to look silly, and exerted his eloquence, in the paragraphs leading up to her death, just because the system had made her a fool:

> In those pleasant little towns on Thames, you may hear the fall of the water over the weirs, or even, in still weather, the rustle of the rushes; and from the bridge you may see the young river, dimpled like a young child, playfully gliding away among the trees, unpolluted by the defilements that lie in wait for it on its course, and as yet

[1] 'The Union' as a synonym for the workhouse was only possible after 1834, and only became generally current in the 'forties.

out of hearing of the deep summons of the sea. It were too much to pretend that Betty Higden made out such thoughts; no; but she heard the tender river whispering to many like herself, 'Come to me, come to me! When the cruel shame and terror you have so long fled from, most beset you, come to me! I am the Relieving Officer appointed by eternal ordinance to do my work; I am not held in estimation according as I shirk it. My breast is softer than the pauper-nurse's; death in my arms is peacefuller than among the pauper-wards. Come to me!' [Book I, Chapter VIII.]

This was written nearly thirty years after *Oliver Twist*: a whole generation had been shamed.

Old Betty Higden, however tired, however footsore, would start up and be driven away by her awakened horror of falling into the hands of Charity. It is a remarkable Christian improvement, to have made a pursuing Fury of the Good Samaritan. [See Note B, p. 105.]

The Postscript, written in lieu of a Preface, to *Our Mutual Friend*, gives Dickens's views of the Poor Law forcibly and finally:

In my social experiences since Mrs. Betty Higden came upon the scene and left it, I have found Circumlocutional champions disposed to be warm with me on the subject of my view of the Poor Law. My friend Mr. Bounderby could never see any difference between leaving the Coketown 'hands' exactly as they were, and requiring them to be fed with turtle soup and venison out of gold spoons. Idiotic propositions of a parallel nature have been freely offered for my acceptance, and I have been called upon to admit that I would give Poor Law relief to anybody, anywhere, anyhow. Putting this nonsense aside, I have observed a suspicious tendency in the champions to divide into two parties; the one contending that there are no deserving Poor who prefer death by slow starvation and bitter weather, to the mercies of some Relieving Officers and some Union Houses; the other admitting that there are such Poor, but denying that they have any cause or reason for what they do. The records in our newspapers, the late exposure by THE LANCET, and the common sense and senses of common people, furnish too abundant evidence against both defences. But, that my view of the Poor Law may not be mistaken or misrepresented, I will state it. I believe there has been in England, since the days of the STUARTS, no law so often infamously administered, no law so often openly violated, no law habitually so ill-supervised. In the majority of the shameful cases of disease and death from destitution that shock the Public and disgrace the country, the illegality is quite equal to the inhumanity—and known language could say no more of their lawlessness.

NOTES TO CHAPTER IV

A. Cf. *Punch*, May 7, 1864. *A Begging Letter from a Bluecoat Boy*: '. . . There was a story out last Christmas that they meant to change our dress, but all they've done is to give us black serge knickerbockers instead of our old corduroy knee-breeches, and they haven't even changed the colour of our stockings. . . . JUVENAL says that poverty makes chaps look ridiculous, and if he had but seen our gowns and yellow stockings, I'm sure he would have said that charity does the same.'

B. From countless examples of Poor Law severity even in the 'sixties one may be quoted which occurred while Dickens was first planning *Our Mutual Friend*. In October 1862, at the inquest on Charlotte Crippin, who had died of starvation, the Coroner stated that 'It was clear that the deceased and her family, being in extreme starvation, presented herself at the union-house. . . . They were placed in a room and there had to undergo such dreadful starvation that deceased died of the effects, and they would have all perished had not their groans attracted the attention of the neighbours.'

CHAPTER V

RELIGION

ONE of the features of English Liberalism in the nineteenth century which most distinguished it from its counterparts in other countries of Europe was the habitual use of Christian language. What was called Infidelity took many forms of opposition to practices and dogmas, but it was hardly ever atheism or agnosticism, and rarely abandoned the Christian name. Tom Paine, a convinced deist, had little lasting popular influence; Richard Carlile still less. Even Robert Owen who seemed, alike to the orthodox Tory and the evangelical fanatic, not far removed from the Beast of the Revelation, often wrote and spoke as if he were restoring pure Christianity in his 'Religion of Charity unconnected with Faith'.

In the period of agitation for Parliamentary Reform between the battle of Waterloo and 1832, religious forms of thought were as common as later with some of the leading Chartists. During the worst years of the Liverpool oppression, though the ministers of the chief Nonconformist bodies, Baptist and Methodist, frequently expressed their loyalty to the existing administration, many of their followers were prominent among the Radicals, while several Independent and Unitarian ministers were popular speakers at meetings for Reform. At Middleton in Lancashire the Reformers hired a chapel where reformist sermons were preached in service-time on Sundays, in which religion and politics were inextricably mixed. The Female Reformers of Manchester issued a manifesto in which Jesus Christ was declared to be the greatest Reformer of all. In 1817 a pamphlet

was published by Elijah Dixon, of which the full title ran:

The Voice of God!!! In support of the Grand Object of Parliamentary Reform. O ye Noblemen, Clergymen, Gentlemen, Tradesmen, Working Men, and Poor Men, of Great Britain, and Ireland, Hear ye the word of the LORD.

By their fruits ye shall know THEM.
CHRIST

It then applied *Nehemiah*, Chapter V, verses 1–19 as 'a complete justification of the Reformers and their Principles'. These are not exceptional instances of sectarian fanaticism or mere eccentricity: the whole movement was saturated with religious, Christian feeling. Speakers in every part of the country drew their quotations and their imagery from the Bible. A similar spirit, moreover, informed the most bitter denunciations of the established Church, the wealthy bishops, the pluralists, the sinecurists, the parson-justices: the Bible and the *Black Book* could be read together. This was the spirit, too, which produced and enjoyed Hone's parodies of the Creed and Litany; and Hone himself, tried and acquitted three times for blasphemy, showed in his great defences that he was a pious as well as a learned man.

But these reformers were not theologically minded: by origin most of them were Dissenters—some Baptists, some Independents, others Methodists of the second or third generation; a few belonged to the Established Church. Yet in the religious language they used they never spoke the peculiar idioms of the sects, nor mentioned their distinguishing doctrines. They were latitudinarian, without having worked out any Biblical justification for being so; nor, of course, had their religion any affinities with the reasoned latitudinarianism of the Church: they cared no more for the doctrines of Paley than for his politics. It is easier to say what their religion was not than to say what it was; but running through it all was the attempt to apply the morality of the Gospels to the state of England—Christ's mercy, his love for the poor, the wickedness of pride in the rich and of sin in high places. A reform sermon was preached on

> Luke 16, 19, and following virses
> Two oposit Caracters are presented to us
> in one welth in the other misery
> yet this was an object of favour while the
> rich man was that of divine disapprobation.
> [*Home Office Papers*, 40.9,1817.]

It would be a mistake to suppose that this sort of religion was confined to illiterate or inarticulate men; it was spread more widely and better understood than the professional religious writers would suggest. Samuel Bamford's two volumes of autobiography, for instance, written in the 'thirties and 'forties but referring to an earlier time, reflect a mood of sincere and very liberal Christianity. It would be easy to show that his language is Socinian; but he was not enough concerned about theological niceties to make the serious social gesture of attending Mr. Gaskell at the Unitarian Chapel in Cross Street. Here are some extracts from his plan of Christian education for the young:

> In every heart there is at least one germ of goodness. I would cultivate that, by every gentle, and kind, and appropriate means; making its practice and development become a pleasure, not less than a duty. . . . I would, with God's help, train up the tender-hearted child to be just, the just one to be merciful, the veracious one to add graciousness to truth, the heroic one to be moderate in triumph, and the magnanimous one to be powerful as well as endurant. In every assemblage of youth, all these good qualities are to be found, like gems strewed in darkness. Why should they

be left to be lost? Precious emanations are they of God's own being. Let us worship God by deeming his gifts worthy of our care—most solicitous care. Children would understand this kind of religion better; they would love it better, they would imbibe it sooner, than the present one

> Of sermonizing and catechising,
> And bell-ringing, and drone-singing,
> And knee-bowing, and pride-showing,
> Of vain finery, and mock shinery.

I would not have it all lip-worship, and form-worship; but heart-worship, coming from the heart, and heart-penetrative, wherever it was introduced. I would, in fact, have less of priestianity, and more of Christ's own Christianity; less of creeds and dogmas, and more of the living faith which bringeth forth works, testifying to the reality of a true belief.

[*Early Days*, Chapter XIII.]

The extent to which such opinions were prevalent in the country cannot be measured from the theologians. The work of such men as Copleston and Whately anticipated that of Arnold; the Whiggery of Sydney Smith kept alive some of the more admirable qualities of eighteenth-century churchmanship; but the typical mid-Victorian Broad Church parson does not come upon the scene until the 'forties, when the Tractarian controversies had given an entirely fresh impulse to theological thought. It is only after the Colenso episode and the publication of *Essays and Reviews* that one can properly speak of a Broad Church Party. Though many of the most vigorous and pious minds, both before and after Dickens began to write, were leading opinion along narrow ways, and though more liberal thought moved slowly, yet there were many lay people in every class willing to entertain Christian sentiment uncorseted by dogma. To such people Dickens appealed; and he increased their number. In fact, one of the chief causes of his success as a

popular moralist and reformer was the skill with which
he struck a good religious note without committing
himself beyond the common stock of Christian phrases.
On the one side he avoided the tone and idiom of any
theological party, and on the other he escaped (at
least in general opinion) the even greater danger of
seeming, like Robert Owen, to recommend a Charity
which was 'unconnected with faith'. If he had done
so with deliberate cynicism he might have succeeded
just as well as he did with Stiggins and Chadband, with
Mrs. Nubbles's Little Bethel, Mrs. Cruncher's flopping
and the Rev. Melchisedech Howler, but he would hardly
have created the Milveys in *Our Mutual Friend* (who
almost alone in his books show the working of a well-
run parish) or Mr. Crisparkle, and he certainly could
never have composed the variations on the Lord's
Prayer which mollify so painfully the end of Jo.

The Established Church is firmly built into the
Dickens landscape. Arthur Clennam may fume at
Sunday bells, remembering the awful Sundays of his
boyhood; weddings like that of Mr. Dombey and Edith
may be designed to make a blessing hideous; the long
train of funerals, with crape and plumes and brandied
mutes, winding to graveyards that pollute the water
and the air, may tarnish the beauty of an orthodox
death; but still, when virtue and truth require a special
burst of eloquence, he returns again and again to the
scenes and forms and language of the Church. The
burden of his *Chimes* is holy and benign. David
Copperfield sets off the churchyard seen from his bed-
room window against the grim Murdstone piety; Tom
Pinch at the organ (a very Anglican figure) plays
preludes and fugues of reproach to the hypocrisy of
Pecksniff; Little Dorrit, after a cold wet night in the
streets at last gets a bed in a vestry; Little Nell
becomes a church mouse. A theologian would find
little in all this to justify the claim that Dickens was

a Christian; a historian could hardly gather from his books that during the years in which they were written the English Church was revolutionized. But the Church was for Dickens a national depository of good-feeling: its establishment allowed for a kind of ancestor-worship, its creeds began with the Father-hood of God. The more mysterious doctrines of Redemption and Grace concerned him very little, the technique of worship not at all.

> O brother man, fold to thy heart thy brother:
> Where pity dwells, the peace of God is there;
> To worship rightly is to love each other,
> Each smile a hymn, each kindly deed a prayer.

His religion is emphatically one of works, not faith; but there is no dwelling on any religious merit works may win. Heaven is more a compensation than a prize. Yet virtue is not purely its own reward: the beneficent characters have their full return in watching the happiness they distribute, and in the enjoyment of gratitude and power. Even Arthur Clennam, who appears in the first part of *Little Dorrit* as the most disinterested doer of good, though working with the vague idea of making amends for an old wrong (his motives are obscure), and who is met with the bitter rude ingratitude of Tip and the sly patronage of Old Dorrit, finds first some return in that Cavalletto was 'so grateful (for little enough)' and finally a triumphant reward in his wife. The Christmas spirit of good-fellowship and kindness wins worldly returns as surely as it expresses itself in worldly goods. Metaphors from money—payment, debt, return—are abnormally common in Dickens's moral language.

Virtue is for him the natural state of man, and happiness its concomitant. 'We can all do some good,' says David Copperfield, 'if we will.' The word 'natural' often slips into Dickens's sentences without thought;

111

but in the great set pieces where the moral condition of the world is reviewed he always adopts the view that man as the child of a good father is himself good, and that the evils of the world are obstructions which prevent him from being himself. He rejected Original Sin. In fact, 'sin' is scarcely mentioned at all.[1] Martha in Chapter XLVII of *David Copperfield* speaks of repentance, but neither she nor David nor Mr. Peggotty says it is 'sin' she must repent of. Edith expects repentance of Mr. Dombey, but she does not say that he has sinned. Evil is always terrifyingly real; but the source of it is obscure. In the earlier novels, especially, the bad characters have a concentrated personal malignity which comes near to making them the devil; Quilp is over and over again called a fiend; there seems to be no redeeming strain of goodness in them; but we never understand how they have escaped the beneficent attention of their Father. In the later novels, a stronger impersonal evil, created by society, works by their side. The Devil and Hell are frequently referred to in passing, but ambiguously; they might be either literal or metaphorical, so that details of belief are left open.

The value of this peculiar form of religion was recognized early in America:

> He shows us, more clearly than any other author whom we can name, what Fancy, baptized with a truly Christian spirit, may achieve towards reconciling man to man, and, through love of the brother whom we have seen, towards leading us to the purer love of the Father, whom we have not seen. [*The Christian Examiner*, Boston, March 1842.]

In England a similar approval appeared in the obituary notice in *Fraser's Magazine*, July 1870:

> He spent no thought on religious doctrines or religious reforms, but regarded the Sermon on the Mount as good teaching, had a regard for the village church and churchyard, and quarrelled with nothing but intolerance.

[1] "Acton once said that Dickens knew nothing of sin when it was not crime."— E. L. Woodward, *The Age of Reform*, p. 535.

Even the Bishop of Manchester, preaching in Westminster Abbey three days after his death, said of him:

> I am sure I have felt in myself the healthful spirit of his
> teaching. Possibly we might not have been able to subscribe
> to the same creed in relation to God, but I think we should
> have subscribed to the same creed in relation to man. He
> who taught us our duty to our fellow-men better than we
> knew it before . . . must be regarded by those who recognize
> the diversity of the gifts of the spirit as a teacher sent from
> God. He would have been welcomed as a fellow-labourer
> in the common interests of humanity by Him who asked the
> question, 'If a man love not his brother whom he hath seen,
> how can he love God whom he hath not seen?'

But by 1870 theologians had travelled a long and
difficult way; thirty years earlier opinion had not been
so easy and generous. The orthodox had then found,
not surprisingly, a good deal to complain of. *The
Christian Remembrancer* for December 1842 had said:

> His religion, whenever any is introduced, is for the most part
> such mere pagan sentimentalism, that we should have been
> better pleased by its absence. . . . The Clergy are never
> introduced otherwise than with a sneer.

The religious satire in *Pickwick* had brought so many
complaints that the later preface had to reassure
readers that religion was not only mentioned to be
ridiculed. This is hardly to be wondered at when we
think of Mr. Weller's first account of his wife's dealings
with the shepherd:

> 'She's been gettin' rayther in the Methodistical order
> lately, Sammy; and she is uncommon pious, to be sure. She's
> too good a creetur for me, Sammy. I feel I don't deserve
> her.'
> 'Ah,' said Mr. Samuel, 'that's wery self-denyin' o' you.'
> 'Wery,' replied his parent, with a sigh. 'She's got hold o'
> some inwention for grown-up people being born again,

Sammy; the new birth, I think they calls it. I should
wery much like to see that system in haction, Sammy.
I should wery much like to see your mother-in-law born
again. Wouldn't I put her out to nurse!'

[Chapter XXII.]

A joke as broad as this on a point of doctrine, not yet
connected with any sanctimoniousness in a character,
and a doctrine, moreover, found so easily in the Bible,
suggests a clever journalist playing up to the drunk
Church-and-King mobs hired to jeer at Wesleyans or
Painites, and it is one of the rare instances in Dickens's
novels of that sheer cock-a-snook vulgarity which
peeps out at times in his letters.[1] It is also oddly out
of keeping with the rest of the Stiggins theme, which,
broadly treated as it is, had solid justification in fact.

An excellent commentary on the evangelical cant
and humbug which Dickens satirized is to be found in
John Foster's *Essay on Some of the Causes by which
Evangelical Religion has been rendered unacceptable to
Persons of cultivated Taste.* Foster was a Baptist
minister, clear-headed, articulate and outspoken, yet
an ardent believer in the distinguishing doctrines of
Evangelicalism in whatever sect they appeared. This
essay, first published in 1805 and in its eighth edition
in 1826, deals mainly with the conflict between Christ
and Apollo, but it also looks through the eyes of an
educated person of taste, sympathetic to Christianity
though not 'converted', at various practices of Evangelicalism. Here is the reaction of such a man to a
Stiggins:

> The religious habits of some Christians may have disgusted
> him excessively. Everything which could even distantly
> remind him of grimace, would inevitably do this; as, for
> instance, a solemn lifting up of the eyes, artificial impulses
> of the breath, grotesque and regulated gestures and postures

[1] Even responsible Churchmen were capable of crude sneers at this particular
doctrine. See, for instance, *Quarterly Review*, Vol. 2, p. 81.

in religious exercises, an affected faltering of the voice, and, I might add, abrupt religious exclamations in common discourse, though they were even benedictions to the Almighty, which he has often heard so ill-timed as to have an irreverent and almost ludicrous effect. In a mind such as I am supposing, the happiest improvement in point of veneration for genuine religion will produce no tolerance still for such habits. Nor will the dislike to them be lessened by ever so perfect a conviction of the sincere piety of any of the persons who have fallen into them.

Coming from Foster this is proof enough that the externals of Stiggins were hardly exaggerated, however unlikely his gross hypocrisy may have been.

Foster then goes on to consider a fault which is peculiarly that of Chadband: the man of taste, he says, has perhaps frequently heard in the conversation of illiterate Christians

the most unfortunate metaphors and similes, employed to explain or enforce evangelical sentiments; and probably, if he twenty times recollected one of those sentiments, or if he heard a similar one from some other quarter, the repulsive figure was sure to recur to his imagination. If he has heard so many of these that each Christian topic has acquired its appropriate images, you can easily conceive what a lively perception of the importance of the subject itself must be requisite to overcome the disgust and banish the associations. The feeling accompanying these topics, as connected with these ideas, will be somewhat like that which spoils the pleasure of reading a noble poet, Virgil for instance, when each admired passage recalls the images into which it has been degraded in that kind of imitation denominated *travesty*. It may be added, that the reluctance to think of the subject because it is connected with these ideas, strengthens that connexion. For often the earnest wish not to dwell on the disagreeable images, produces a mischievous reaction by which they press in more forcibly. . . .

. . . I cannot help wishing that religious teachers were aware of the propriety of not amplifying the less dignified

class of those metaphors which it may be proper enough
sometimes to introduce, and which perhaps are employed,
in a short and transient way, in the Bible.

Let Chadband speak:

> I say this brother, present here among us, is devoid of
> parents, devoid of relations, devoid of flocks and herds,
> devoid of gold, of silver, and of precious stones, because he
> is devoid of the light that shines in upon some of us. . . . I
> ask you what is that light? . . . It is the ray of rays, the sun
> of suns, the moon of moons, the star of stars. It is the light
> of Terewth. . . . Say not to me that it is *not* the lamp of
> lamps. I say to you, it is. I say to you, a million times
> over, it is.

The habit of distending such commonplace com-
parisons was so ingrained in evangelical speech that
one of the evangelists of the Home Missionary Society
devised a sort of parlour-game called Church Questions,
'for the purpose of creating in his little flock a spirit of
inquiry after truth, and to induce them to search the
Scriptures. At every monthly meeting, the answers to
the last question are given by each member, and the
next question is proposed. The questions are all
founded on Scripture, and the answers have the
explanatory texts appended to them. From the whole
is collected an instructive and pleasing train of illus-
trations.' For example:

> *Question:*—In what respects do the people of God resemble
> jewels. *Founded on Mal.* III, 7.
> *Answer:*—In their origin.—In their great rarity.—In their
> beauty.—In their shining quality.—In their preciousness.—
> In their durability.—In being ornamental.—In their value
> being frequently determined by their weight.—In not being
> susceptible of injury by passing through a moderate fire.
> [Quoted in *Quarterly Review*, Vol. 32, p. 26, 1825.]

It is easy to see how the use of such language—still

more the playing of such a game—induces hypocrisy. The associations proceed from word to word, ever moving farther from the original point of reference; and a habit of association once formed may proceed in indefinite triumph with no point of reference at all. Chadband was a hypocrite at Snagsby's tea-party because he had not stopped to think whether his words had any reference to the facts about Jo.

I must quote Foster once more:

> The usual language of hypocrisy, at least of vulgar hypocrisy, is cant; and religious cant is often an affected use of the phrases which have been heard employed as appropriate to evangelical truth; with which phrases the hypocrite has connected no distinct ideas, so that he would be confounded if a sensible examiner were to require an accurate explanation of them; while yet nothing is more easy to be sung or said. Now were this diction, for the greater part, to vanish from Christian society, leaving the truth in its mere essence behind, and were, consequently, the pretender reduced to assume the guise of religion on the wide and laborious plan of acquiring an understanding of its leading principles, so as to be able to assign them discriminatively in language of his own; the part of a hypocrite would be much less easily acted, and less frequently attempted. Religion would therefore be seldomer dishonoured by the mockery of a false semblance.

If any such reform in the 'technical terms' of religion as that which Foster recommends in this essay had come about, the whole religious history of the nineteenth century would have been altered; and in particular Dickens's own religious language, which now seems commonplace to us, would not then have come to his public with such freshness and originality. For it is only necessary to compare any of his religious passages with similar passages in the professedly religious fiction of the time to see at once what a relief his idiom must have been, even for the most pious, from the distinctive jargon which had accrued round holy things.[1]

In a story called *The Merchant's Fortune*, published by the Religious Tract Society in 1849, we can see the fate of a Dombey or a Veneering through other eyes:

> Forty years of toil for gain, unsanctified by hopes beyond the gold, and wishes beyond the self-indulgence it may buy, will leave only their godless record for the eternal condemnation of the sinner at the judgment day.
>
> Pause then, young beginners in this world's absorbing business, and begin with God. . . .

Compare this with the moral put in Edith Dombey's mouth when she is talking to Florence:

> When he loves his Florence most, he will hate me least. When he is most proud and happy in her and her children, he will be most repentant of his own part in the dark vision of our married life. At that time, I will be repentant too—let him know it then—and think that when I thought so much of all the causes that had made me what I was, I needed to have allowed more for the causes that had made him what he was. I will try, then, to forgive him his share of blame. Let him try to forgive me mine!

Or here is Dickens in an avowedly pious mood:

> Then, as Christmas is a time in which, of all times in the year, the memory of every remediable sorrow, wrong, and trouble in the world around us, should be active with us, not less than our own experiences, for all good, he laid his hand upon the boy, and silently calling Him to witness who laid His hand on children in old time, rebuking, in the majesty of His prophetic knowledge, those who kept them from Him, vowed to protect him, teach him, reclaim him.
>
> [*The Haunted Man.*]

---

[1] His ear for religious clichés was wonderfully quick. Mrs. Pardiggle saying as early as 1853 that the Matins to which she took the children was 'very prettily done', used a phrase which may be heard to-day in any of the streets between St. Stephen's, Gloucester Road, and St. Augustine's, Queen's Gate.

Compare another Religious Tract Society story:

> These dear little children are only entrusted to the parent's
> care for a season, but they are to be trained for eternity.
> God declares that they are His 'heritage' (Psalm cxxvii, 3).
> Parents therefore have no right to abuse them. Children
> were the subject of the peculiar interest of our Lord Jesus
> Christ, and He Himself bids us take heed how we 'offend'
> them by our cruel or unjust treatment. 'Forbid them not to
> come unto Me,' said our Lord when on earth; then, parents,
> permit your children to attend the teacher who will tell
> them of this blessed Saviour's love. If you cannot lay up
> for them treasures on earth, oh permit them to seek those
> true riches which perish not, but will afford them comfort
> and happiness when this world and the fashion of it shall
> have passed away.

It is of course unfair to put such quotations side by
side if the purpose is merely to show that Dickens, not
by a long way near his best, is better than an anonymous
nonentity treating the same subject, considering as
coolly as we can by such standards as we have. But
it is fair to suppose that a pious person might have read
both on the same day when both were still new, and
to wonder what reverberations were set going by the
difference of idiom.

Many, it must be confessed, would have frankly
preferred the nonentity, so ingrained was that style
in the ordinary evangelical mind. And it is hardly to
be wondered at that the evangelical press attacked
Dickens not only for his satire but also for the absence
in his work of any doctrinal language and the almost
total absence of church-going of a proper public kind.
But perhaps more important than this was the fact
that none of his good characters acted from an overt
religious motive: it gave great offence to some that the
Pickwick-Cheeryble kind of benevolence was not God-
directed in a conscious way. And the goodness of the
good young women too, though punctuated at intervals

with heartfelt prayers, sprang more from natural niceness than from the constant visits to the closet recommended by *The Young Lady's Guide*.

The heroine of a thorough evangelical novel only begins her career of moral improvement at the point where one of Dickens's good young women would leave off. Here, for instance, is Ellen Seymour on page 15:[1]

> Her education had, as we have before observed, been most carefully conducted; while no pains had been spared to ensure the cultivation of her talents, no less had been the attention bestowed on her moral training, and the result was, as might have been expected, the formation of a character exhibiting one of the most perfect specimens of natural beauty and attractiveness. Happy in herself, the delight of her parents and all around her, Ellen's life had been, till within the last few months, one bright scene of uninterrupted felicity. Towards God, as the author of her existence, and all her blessings, her heart went forth in feelings of grateful adoration. She was an ardent lover of the beauties of nature, and in the loveliness of creation she discovered, as she imagined, the love of God the Creator; but here she stopped. She never thought of the infinite love of God, and of his almighty power and holiness, as displayed in the incarnation, sufferings, death, and resurrection, of his only begotten Son. No; the history of redemption she had been taught to acknowledge as an article of belief, and to view it as conferring some inestimable benefit on the whole of the human race, in which she believed herself, as a matter of course, included, but of a personal and individual interest in the great plan of salvation she neither felt nor knew the necessity.

The outline of her external history is roughly parallel to that of Bella Wilfer, for it culminates in a marriage which makes it possible to relieve her father from poverty; but whereas Bella is 'converted' from being a mercenary little wretch into a girl who marries the

[1] *Ellen Seymour; or, The Bud and the Flower*, by Mrs. Savile Shepherd (Anne Houlditch), 1848, (7th ed., 1858). Also contains anti-Tractarian propaganda.

unknown John Rokesmith for love, Ellen is converted
to the full evangelical faith, and marries a clergyman,
who has, unknown to her, the necessary nest-egg.

Dickens's deep and bitter hatred of evangelicalism
in its most malignant forms was not usually directed
against any of its typical Christian doctrines. It is
very surprising, on looking through *David Copperfield*
carefully, to find how little is actually said about the
Murdstones' religion. The overburdening effect of it
all through the book derives almost entirely from the
single paragraph in Chapter IV beginning: 'The gloomy
taint that was in the Murdstone blood, darkened the
Murdstone religion, which was austere and wrathful.'
It describes the church-going, with Miss Murdstone
'emphasizing all the dread words with a cruel relish'
and the lasting effect of it depends as much as on
anything on the one fact of her poking David during
the service with her Prayer Book till his sides ached.
Scarcely a word is said again of their religion till
Chapter LIX when David, coming back from abroad,
runs by chance into Mr. Chillip.

> 'Mrs. Chillip,' he proceeded, in the calmest and slowest
> manner, 'quite electrified me, by pointing out that Mr.
> Murdstone sets up an image of himself, and calls it the
> Divine Nature. . . . The ladies are great observers, sir?'
> 'Intuitively,' said I, to his extreme delight. . . .
> 'Mrs. Chillip does go so far as to say,' pursued the meekest
> of little men, much encouraged, 'that what such people
> miscall their religion, is a vent for their bad humours and
> arrogance. And do you know I must say, sir,' he continued,
> mildly laying his head on one side, 'that I *don't* find authority
> for Mr. and Miss Murdstone in the New Testament?'
> 'I never found it either,' said I.

From this it is clear that the bullying and avaricious
character comes first, and the religion follows as a
subsequent justification of it. This was a common
development in certain forms of extreme Protestantism

for two main reasons. The acceptance of the whole Bible as equally and wholly the exact word of God put the Old Testament on a par with the New, and made it possible for those who preferred to do so to draw their morality from the sternest parts of the non-Christian books. It is amazing to see how even piously gentle people were prepared to do this when it was convenient. When Charlotte Elizabeth started a Protestant Sunday School for Irish boys she acted on this plan of Bible reading without the slightest doubts of its wisdom:

> Our choice of chapters was peculiar. I found they wanted stirring subjects, and I gave them Gideon, Samson, Jonathan, Nehemiah, Boaz, Mordecai, Daniel, and all the most manly characters of Old Testament history, with the rich gospel that lies wrapped in every page of that precious volume . . . really my little lads became gentlemen in mind and manners, while, blessed be God! not a few became, I trust, wise unto salvation.

The difficulty was how to extract and refine the 'rich gospel': with an almost literal acceptance of the text it was possible to use the Old Testament to justify almost anything, and not merely to justify it, but to indulge all the arrogance and self-righteousness in the identification of personal desires with the will of God. The supposed infallibility of a book thus combined with the supposed infallibility of a twice-born judgement.

The way this process worked is seen best in Mrs. Clennam. Religion had no part in Dickens's original conception of her; it was added afterwards to enforce in a more effective and gloomy way the idea of a wicked old woman fond of power, concealing her misdeeds; the effect of her training on Arthur was what might have happened to David if he had not run away. For the evil force of such religion was greatest on children, and it was partly Dickens's insight into childhood that attracted him to it. It contained the worst distortion of the idea of Fatherhood upon which his own religion was based.

The misery of oppression was concentrated on Sundays. Arthur Clennam sat in the coffee-house on Ludgate Hill on the Sunday morning of his return to London, listening to the last monotonous bell until it stopped:

Its sound had revived a long train of miserable Sundays, and the procession would not stop with the bell, but continued to march on. 'Heaven forgive me,' said he, 'and those who trained me. How I have hated this day!'

There was the dreary Sunday of his childhood, when he sat with his hands before him, scared out of his senses by a horrible tract which commenced business with the poor child by asking him in its title, why he was going to Perdition?— a piece of curiosity that he really in a frock and drawers was not in a condition to satisfy—and which, for the further attraction of his infant mind, had a parenthesis in every other line with some such hiccupping reference as 2 Ep. Thess., c. iii, v. 6 & 7. There was the sleepy Sunday of his boyhood, when, like a military deserter, he was marched to chapel by a picquet of teachers three times a day, morally handcuffed to another boy; and when he would willingly have bartered two meals of indigestible sermon for another ounce or two of inferior mutton at his scanty dinner in the flesh. There was the interminable Sunday of his nonage; when his mother, stern of face and unrelenting of heart, would sit all day behind a Bible—bound, like her own construction of it, in the hardest, barest, and straitest boards, with one dinted ornament on the cover like the drag of a chain, and a wrathful sprinkling of red upon the edges of the leaves—as if it, of all books! were a fortification against sweetness of temper, natural affection, and gentle intercourse. There was the resentful Sunday of a little later, when he sat glowering and glooming through the tardy length of the day, with a sullen sense of injury in his heart, and no more real knowledge of the beneficent history of the New Testament, than if he had been bred among idolaters.

123

It was possibly this sympathy with childhood that made Dickens see also how Sunday could be used by the upper classes as a means of oppressing the lower. His early paper called *Sunday Under Three Heads*, written against Sir Andrew Agnew's Sunday Observance Bill in 1836, contains nothing more effective than the demonstration how every single restriction—on travelling, shopping, amusements, etc.—that the Bill sought to impose was a restriction only on the poorer classes. The rich retained on the seventh day as 'necessary', because normal, their carriages, footmen, huge meals served by servants and so on; but for the poor any kind of travel and enjoyment was to be damned and forbidden as 'unnecessary' just because they had not the leisure or the money for such things on the other six days of the week. Sunday was thus to be used as another means of keeping the people down and enforcing the 'prudence' and economy already advocated by the Malthusian politicians.[1]

The idea of a conservative Providence, concerned to maintain the existing social divisions and distribution of property was, of course, familiar enough from many writers; familiar also was the exaltation of the advantages and blessings of poverty as a means of allaying discontent. On this point the arguments of Paley in 1781 are substantially repeated by Smiles in 1875.[2] But the Providence of Malthus appeared not merely conservative but positively malignant. He had, of course, given his theory religious support. He argued that 'the great Author of Nature', 'by making the passion of self-love beyond comparison stronger than the passion of benevolence' has 'impelled us to that line of conduct, which is essential to the preservation

---

[1] cf. *The Sunday Screw*, 1850.

[2] Compare Paley's *Reasons for Contentment, Addressed to the Labouring Part of the British Public* with Chapter XIV of Smiles's *Thrift*. But while Paley argues that the poor man is out and out more likely to be happy than the rich, Smiles, by a typical paradox, says a chief happiness of poverty lies in the struggle not to be poor.

of the human race'. It was thus God's intention to *make* men restrict relief to the poor, and inculcate restraints on breeding: prudence, thrift, and chastity were enforced by the limitation of the fertility of the soil. Dr. Thomas Chalmers, one of the most popular Early Victorian divines, was also a Malthusian.

Dickens's advocacy of spending, of 'the amusements of the people', especially on their only free day, of the physical pleasure of the poor, was thus also part of his religious belief that the scheme of the world was kindly and men fundamentally good, in opposition to the view that life was little but a gloomy warfare against evil and misery. This belief would naturally find expression in what he thought to be an ideal Sunday, and such a day is described in the last part of *Sunday Under Three Heads*. Its scene (as one would expect of a good Cockney) is a small village in the West. The morning is bright and pleasant, the hedges green and blooming; there are stout young labourers in clean round frocks, and buxom girls with healthy, laughing faces. The little church is half overgrown with moss and ivy, and the very letters from its monuments are worn away. Then the service:

> The impressive service of the Church of England was spoken—not merely *read*—by a grey-headed minister, and the responses delivered by his auditors, with an air of sincere devotion as far removed from affectation or display as from coldness or indifference. The psalms were accompanied by a few instrumental performers, who were stationed in a small gallery extending across the church at the lower end, over the door: and the voices were led by the clerk, who it was evident derived no slight pride and gratification from this part of the service. The discourse was plain, unpretending, and well adapted to the comprehension of the hearers.

The clergyman makes kindly conversation as the people come out; and in the evening a cricket-match is played in the clergyman's own field with stumps, bats, and ball provided by himself.

This is the scene that Dickens as a young man would have liked to see repeated all over the country and especially round London on every summer Sunday. It was described before the revivalist propaganda of Young England began, and before the Oxford Movement had entered on its aesthetic and ritualistic phase. Dickens's ideal remained unchanged throughout his life, untouched by any influence from the new medievalism which in a thousand ways was modifying the religion, the art, and even—in such things as Gothic railway-stations—the practical life of England. He wanted a brighter world; he hated the gloom of Little Bethel; but he recoiled in almost neurotic horror from all the most vigorous and original work that aimed to bring colour and form back into art and religion. Pre-Raphaelites and Puseyites were equally targets for his scorn. Here, for instance, is his verdict on *The Carpenter's Shop* by Millais:

You come—in this Royal Academy Exhibition, which is familiar with the works of Wilkie, Collins, Etty, Eastlake, Mulready, Leslie, Maclise, Turner, Stanfield, Landseer, Roberts, Danby, Creswick, Lee, Webster, Herbert, Dyce, Cope, and others who would have been renowned as great masters in any age or country—you come, in this place, to the contemplation of a Holy Family. You will have the goodness to discharge from your minds all Post-Raphael ideas, all religious aspirations, all elevating thoughts; all tender, awful, sorrowful, ennobling, sacred, graceful, or beautiful associations; and to prepare yourselves, as befits such a subject—Pre-Raphaelly considered—for the lowest depths of what is mean, odious, repulsive, and revolting.

You behold the interior of a carpenter's shop. In the foreground of that carpenter's shop is a hideous, wry-necked, blubbering, red-headed boy, in a bed-gown; who appears to have received a poke in the hand, from the stick of another boy with whom he has been playing in an adjacent gutter,

126

and to be holding it up for the contemplation of a kneeling
woman, so horrible in her ugliness, that (supposing it were
possible for any human creature to exist for a moment with
that dislocated throat) she would stand out from the rest
of the company as a Monster, in the vilest cabaret in France,
or the lowest gin-shop in England. Two almost naked
carpenters, master and journeyman, worthy companions of
this agreeable female, are working at their trade; a boy,
with some small flavour of humanity in him, is entering with
a vessel of water; and nobody is paying any attention to a
snuffy old woman who seems to have mistaken that shop
for the tobacconist's next door, and to be hopelessly waiting
at the counter to be served with half an ounce of her favourite
mixture. Wherever it is possible to express ugliness of
feature, limb, or attitude, you have it expressed. Such men
as the carpenters might be undressed in any hospital where
dirty drunkards, in a high state of varicose veins, are received.
Their very toes have walked out of Saint Giles's.

[*Old Lamps for New Ones.*]

He then castigates the Academy for 'attaching greater
weight

to mere handicraft, than to any other consideration—even
to considerations of common reverence or decency; which
absurd principle, in the event of a skilful painter of the
figure becoming a very little more perverted in his taste,
than certain skilful painters are just now, might place Her
Gracious Majesty in a very painful position, one of these fine
Private View Days.'

It is scarcely possible to believe that such a crazy
judgement was ever made, except on the assumption
that Dickens had seen only the reproduction of the
picture in the *Illustrated London News*; yet other critics
said similar things—*Punch*, for instance, diagnosed in
the Holy Family 'scrofular or strumous diathesis'—
and the picture evidently touched some obscure deep-
rooted prejudices in the British public which Dickens
fully shared. For all that he insisted so much on the

127

'humanity' of Christ, he evidently disliked the idea that
he or his family had any of the ordinary physical imperfections of humans; and the suggestion of a little dirt,
even in a carpenter's shop, was unwelcome to a generation that was preaching a loud gospel of personal
cleanliness; the Holy Family had to appear respectable
even if their clothes were quaint. But deeper than
these was the suspicion of asceticism, of the idea that
there was some integral connexion between the lean
sinewy figures and the goodness of their possessors.
1850, the year in which the picture was exhibited, was
also the year of the 'Papal Aggression'. The Pope had
declared his intention of establishing regular dioceses
in England, and anti-Roman feeling was running high.
Anything that savoured of Romish practices or Romish
ethics was liable to be suspect, and asceticism was such
a thing.[1]

In nothing was Dickens so much of an elementary
John Bull as in his hatred of Roman Catholicism. The
Pope is the real villain of his *Child's History of England*,
and *Pictures from Italy* is full of the most stagey descriptions of visits to the scenes of inquisitional torture.
Monks in the streets are pitied or smiled at, and the
whole system of the Catholic Church is treated as a
cunning imposture. Suspicion of the moral, social, and
political work of Catholicism was not compensated in
his mind by any sympathy for sacramental ideas or
any understanding of the need for spiritual authority.
As a good liberal he thought that the Catholic religion
should be tolerated as one of a number of possible
sects in the nineteenth century, even though it was no
more than a barbarous survival of old superstition: in
Barnaby Rudge he even went so far as to sympathize
with the Catholics because they were persecuted; but
such sympathy did not extend to the renewal of papal

[1] The woodcut which appeared in the *Illustrated London News* is reproduced
beside a modern reproduction from the original by Mr. Paul Oppé in *Early Victorian
England*, II, p. 162; several points in the above paragraph are from his essay.

claims to authority in the realm of England. And perhaps even less did it extend to the Puseyites, whom he regarded as the deluded apes of Rome.

All this might alone be enough to explain why Dickens should have been on the side of the howling crowd against Millais: he might have been just trumping up aesthetic reasons for inveterate religious prejudice;[1] but, in addition, his powers of appreciation of any art were probably more limited and his taste more set and conventional than those of any man of comparable creative genius. His obituary notice in *Fraser's Magazine* rightly pointed out that he had no more liking for painting and music than the average middle-class English gentleman. And he had little more understanding of what these arts could be in the service of religion. 'I am not mechanically acquainted with the art of painting,' he said when faced with the duty of describing Leonardo's *Last Supper*, 'and have no other means of judging of a picture than as I see it resembling and refining upon nature, and presenting graceful combinations of forms and colours.' There could scarcely be a more jejune confession of taste, and it has that attitude of detached connoisseurship which is typical of those who do not realize that in a healthy culture the arts are a normal part of the life of common people. He would not have wished his admired village church to have been decorated with more than an illegible inscription, or have praised a Tractarian Vicar who pulled the ivy off.[2]

His plans for the amusements of the people and for

[1] It is certainly odd that in the long list of painters he approves there should be the names of so many men who had positively influenced the Pre-Raphaelites.

[2] But 'the half murderous and ogreish temper attributed to the ivy [in "The Ivy Green" in *Pickwick*] is a pure bit of common-place. As the ivy is seen in its richest life where there is most decay, it would occur to anyone to depict it as feeding on time and death, and this idea is worked out in every verse. But if that were really the most natural idea suggested, we should regard ivy with more disgust than pleasure . . . and we need not say that that is not really the sentiment with which a plant is regarded that we all cultivate so carefully, and are so glad to see covering bare walls and enveloping the most beautiful and stately of buildings."

[*The Spectator*, December 29, 1877.]

brighter Sundays did, it is true, include the opening
of museums and picture galleries, but rather as a dutiful
acknowledgement that such things could provide harm-
less and 'educational' recreation: art was there stabi-
lized as an honourable deposit from the past. Dickens
understood something, too, of the aesthetic barrenness
and squalor of industrial civilization: this is plainest
in the descriptions in *Hard Times* of the dreary streets
of Coketown and its countless ugly chapels; he approached the beginning of the aesthetic-moral line of
attack on society that became the main work of Ruskin
and Arnold. But he had no conception of a vital
contemporary art which, from religious or any other
motives, should transform the conditions of people's
lives. He himself shared in the emotional deficiency
of the civilization he lived in. The intensive cult of
the elementary domestic affections was partly to com-
pensate for the lack of emotional satisfaction and
stimulus in the wider life of society.

From this point of view the Oxford Movement and
the Catholic revival can be seen as symptoms of the
desire for an outward expression, both in public worship
and in religious art, of the need for an intensified feeling
of community and for something that should enliven
with form and colour and music the drabness of things.
Mrs. Pardiggle's Matins, 'very prettily done', was an
attempt to provide something in social life of which
Dickens himself felt the lack; but he hated formalism,
the suggestion of priestcraft, and the intricacy of
doctrine with all the controversy that it led to. It
might also be added that he instinctively suspected
anything that smacked of 'revival': in his mind the
England of cricket in the clergyman's field had never
died out; it did not need reviving; it merely needed
the chance to keep alive. The idea of resurrecting games
and ceremonies and styles of painting from a remoter
past offended his fundamental belief in progress.

His practical humanist kind of Christianity hardly touched the fringes of what is called religious experience, and his work shows no indication of any powerful feeling connected with a genuinely religious subject. When he came to write a hymn it was a pale and spiritless affair:

> Hear my prayer, O! Heavenly Father,
>   Ere I lay me down to sleep;
> Bid Thy Angels, pure and holy,
>   Round my bed their vigil keep.
>
> My sins are heavy, but Thy mercy
>   Far outweighs them every one;
> Down before Thy Cross I cast them,
>   Trusting in Thy help alone.
>
> Keep me through this night of peril
>   Underneath its boundless shade;
> Take me to Thy rest, I pray Thee,
>   When my pilgrimage is made.
>
> None shall measure out Thy patience
>   By the span of human thought;
> None shall bound the tender mercies
>   Which Thy Holy Son has bought.
>
> Pardon all my past transgressions,
>   Give me strength for days to come;
> Guide and guard me with Thy blessing
>   Till Thy Angels bid me home.[1]

[1] From *The Wreck of the Golden Mary*, Christmas Story, 1856, *Household Words*, Vol. XIV. This hymn was the cause of one of Dickens's characteristic confessions of his faith. A clergyman had written to him about it, not knowing who the author was; Dickens answered on Christmas Eve, 1856: 'I beg to thank you for your very acceptable letter—not the less gratifying to me because I am myself the writer you refer to. . . . There cannot be many men, I believe, who have a more humble veneration for the New Testament, or a more profound conviction of its all-sufficiency, than I have. If I am ever (as you tell me I am) mistaken on this subject, it is because I discountenance all obtrusive professions of and tradings in religion, as one of the main causes why real Christianity has been retarded in this world; and because my observation of life induces me to hold in unspeakable dread and horror, those unseemly squabbles about the letter which drive the spirit out of hundreds of thousands.' [Forster: *Life*, Bk. XI, Chapter III.]

Not a syllable falls out of accepted commonplace; there is hardly a trace of interest even.

But when he uses Christian imagery in describing things about which he did feel deeply it is difficult not to feel that it is a mask to conceal some inability to control or express his emotion. There was no question of deliberate hypocrisy; he accepted certain religious opinions, and thought that they were the proper adjuncts of any emotional crisis; but the emotions were more powerful than the beliefs, and the two could never coalesce. Nearly all his most embarrassing pathos is expressed in religious or semi-religious imagery and terms. The three famous deaths—those of Little Nell, Paul Dombey, and Jo—where modern readers find the uncontrolled squandering of sentiment hard not merely to appreciate, but even to understand, obviously affected Dickens very deeply, as they affected numbers of his readers. But it is significant that the strongest contemporary protests against their pathos came from the religious press. There is a failure to assimilate and dignify the fact of suffering and waste; and the pity in those scenes, especially in the death of Jo, is merely self-pity transferred. The exaggerated consolation that Jo is supposed to extract from the Lord's Prayer (which anyway he could not have understood even so far) not merely degrades the use of it into a kind of private superstition, but also has the mood of somebody in a state of utter emotional collapse enjoying his own prostration and mouthing formulae from another scheme of values as if they expressed his own. Apart from the use of religious terms, it is the pleasurable self-indulgence of these scenes that is so distasteful and, incidentally, so unchristian. Their popularity at the time is partly explained by the fact that a religion in a state of transition from supernatural belief to humanism is very poorly equipped to face death, and must dwell on it for that very reason.

CHAPTER VI

THE CHANGING SCENE

DICKENS lived through the years which saw the making of modern England, and of the middle-class oligarchy which is its government. His boyhood ended with the struggles for Catholic Emancipation and the Reform Bill: his writing life coincided almost exactly with the rule of the Ten-Pound Householders. Middle-class government then meant middle-class reform—the assault on obsolete privileges and procedure, the abolition of restraints on trade, industry, and acquisitiveness, and the painful construction of a legal and administrative system adapted to the conditions which gave the middle classes their power.

The technical achievements of the years between 1812 and 1870 had a far greater effect on those who saw them than any such achievements since: railways altered the whole pattern of the country's life more deeply than cars or aeroplanes. For us, accustomed to ever-accelerating change, it is difficult to recover the mood of mixed utilitarian satisfaction and emotional excitement with which railway, telegraph, and submarine cable were greeted. Our grandfathers were enthralled by such books as Lardner's on the steam-engine and his *Museum of Science and Art* 'illustrated by engravings on wood'. The cuts of cranks and valves provoked them to something like aesthetic enthusiasm; the titbits of astronomy[1] and geology made them think

[1] See letter of Dickens to Mrs. Watson, November 1, 1854: 'I think you will be interested with a controversy between Whewell and Brewster, on the question of the shining orbs about us being inhabited or no. Whewell's book is called, On the Plurality of Worlds; Brewster's, More Worlds than One. . . . They bring together a vast number of points of great interest in natural philosophy, and some very curious reasoning on both sides, and leave the matter pretty much where it was.'

seriously, and often with disastrous results, about the Creation of the World; the chapters on cables and telegraphs urged them irresistibly to quote the boast of Puck. The more thoughtful perhaps shared something of Carlyle's apprehension, first voiced in 1829,[1] that mechanization of external life might mean a baleful mechanization of the mind. But all alike, after a first hesitation or resistance, were compelled to accept the new world and the social changes that it brought: all were part of it, and there was no more escape for Dickens than for anybody else.

Some measure of the changes can be made if we compare *Pickwick* with *Our Mutual Friend*. The books are plainly by the same author; but when all allowances have been made for the obvious differences of form, theme, mood, and setting, for the influence of Dickens's private life upon his art, for developments in his art itself, it still remains clear that the two books are the produce of different climates. It is sometimes said in discussions of Dickens's technique as a novelist that any of his great characters could step out of one book into another without materially disturbing the arrangement of either. But if we try to imagine Sam Weller in *Our Mutual Friend* the limitations of this formal criticism are at once plain. The physique, features, and complexion of the characters have changed between the two books almost as much as their clothes: the grimaces of villains have conformed to a new fashion; manners are so altered that one would as little expect that Boffin should get drunk as that John Harmon should fight a duel. We feel that people use knives and forks in a different style. Everybody is more restrained. The eccentrics and monsters in the earlier books walk through a crowd without exciting particular attention: in the latter they are likely to be pointed at in the streets, and are forced into bitter seclusion; social

[1] *Signs of the Times: Edinburgh Review*, No. 98.

conformity has taken on a new meaning. Silas Wegg and Mr. Venus are at odds and ends with their world as Daniel Quilp was not. The middle classes are more self-important, the lower less self-assured. London, though vastly bigger in extent, is smaller in mystery: it has been opened up by the police. The whole scene seems narrower, more crowded, and, in a peculiar way, more stuffy. The very air seems to have changed in quality, and to tax the powers of Sanitary Reform to the uttermost.[1] In *Pickwick* a bad smell was a bad smell; in *Our Mutual Friend* it is a problem.

These changes cannot be attributed to machinery only, nor to any one cause: but the cumulative effect of difference is so striking that it is impossible to understand Dickens without following in some detail the impact of external changes on his work. Chesterton loved to push him back into the world of Gillray, Rowlandson, and Cobbett, to stress that he 'carries on a rank, rowdy, jolly tradition, of men falling off coaches, before the sons of Science and the Great Exhibition began to travel primly on rails—or grooves'. We have already considered some of the reasons why Dickens wrote so much about the Cobbett world; and one or two quotations showing his early conformity to it may perhaps be the best way of pointing his important later changes. Here is an extract from the *Memoirs* of Henry Hunt, written in 1820 or 1821:

> I could not avoid observing to myself the contrast between the elegant apartment I was now in and that which I had just quitted in Graystock-place; the name Thistlewood was still tinkling upon the drum of my ear, I having quite forgotten where I had heard it before.
>
> In a few minutes two gentlemen walked in; the one dressed in a handsome dressing-gown and morocco slippers, the other in a shabby-genteel black. The former addressed me

[1] This was partly caused by the enormous increase in the use of coal; the London fog in *Our Mutual Friend* is thicker and dirtier even than that in *Bleak House*.

very familiarly by name, saying, that he was Mr. Thistlewood,
and he begged to introduce his friend Dr. Watson.

The Watson family seem to have been generally
accepted as shabby-genteel people; and the Doctor's
son, when wanted in 1817 by the Home Office for his
glorious attempt to capture the Tower of London,
appeared in the official description as a full-dress
Dickens figure, improved by Cruikshank:

> . . . has a mark or mole with a few hairs on it on his Left
> Cheek Bone near the Eye, the left Eyelid rather dropping
> over the Eye, very faint remains of Smallpox in his Face,
> has a rather wide Mouth, and shows his Teeth (which are
> very black) when he laughs; he sometimes wore a Brown
> Great Coat, Black Under Coat, Black Waistcoat, Blue
> Pantaloons, and Hessian Boots; his Appearance shabby
> genteel: He formerly lodged in *Hyde Street, Bloomsbury*.[1]

These people obviously have a close likeness in appearance, dress, and social position to characters in *Pickwick,
Oliver Twist, Nicholas Nickleby*, and *The Old Curiosity
Shop*: the language of the descriptions is, abating genius,
the language of those books. There is, in fact, a closer
likeness between the Watsons and the early Dickens
characters in all externals than between the early
Dickens characters and the later. It is dangerous to
be too exact, but it is clear that in the 'forties a different
style of person comes on the Dickens scene, and that
the scene itself changes. There is a difference of
atmosphere between *A Christmas Carol* (1843), which
is a story of vague undated benevolence, and *The
Chimes* (1844), which is a topical satire. *Martin
Chuzzlewit* is uncertain ground; but it is safe to say
that in *Dombey and Son* the new style is so far
developed as to be unmistakable. The people, places,
and things become 'modern'.

The general chronology of *Dombey* works out quite

---

[1] Home Office Papers, 42, 164.

well if we assume that the book's plot ended with the writing of it in 1848. Florence was then the mother of a son old enough to talk intelligently about his 'poor little uncle': supposing she was then twenty-one or two, Paul would have been born about 1833[1] and died 1840–1. This fits some of the main episodes that can be dated by historical events. The journey of Dombey and the Major to Leamington happened soon after Paul's death: the London and Birmingham Railway, by which they travelled, was fully opened in September 1838, and the Royal Hotel, Leamington, at which they stayed, was pulled down about 1841–2.[2] In describing the Leamington scenes Dickens was obviously drawing on memories of a holiday he had there with Hablot Browne in the autumn of 1838; and Browne was their illustrator. Mr. Carker's death at Paddock Wood station was only possible after 1844, when the branch line was opened from there to Maidstone. The book and the period thus hang together without any serious problems of anachronism. In it there is still a lot from the 1820's. Sol Gills with his decaying, out-of-date business, and even the Dombey firm itself, living on the worn maxim, ill-observed, of a pushing eighteenth-century merchant, are intended to appear as survivals from another age. As a whole the book shows an emotional as well as a practical 'consciousness of living in a world of change', an apprehension of what the changes meant in detail every day, the new quality of life they brought. *Dombey*, more than any of his major works, shows how quickly and surely Dickens could sense the mood of his time, and incorporate new sensations in imaginative literature.

The new mood and atmosphere are very largely caused by the railways: the publication of the book

---

[1] He was not weaned when work began at the London end of the Birmingham Railway—April 1834.

[2] B. W. Matz: *Dickensian Inns and Taverns*, p. 134 ff.

coincided with the railway mania of the middle 'forties.[1]
It would be hard to exaggerate the effect of those years
on English social life. Practically the whole country
was money-mad; the public attitude to investment was
quite altered, and it then first became clear that Joint
Stock companies, however imperfectly managed, were
certain to become a permanent and influential feature
of finance. Railway works helped to absorb the unemployed and so to remove the fear of revolution. The
growth of home consumption was enormously acceler-
ated by improved transport: diet, furniture, fireplaces,
and all the physical appurtenances of life changed
character more rapidly; the very landscape was given
a new aesthetic character—even perhaps a new standard[2]—by embankments, cuttings, and viaducts. But,
above all, the scope and tempo of individual living were
revolutionized, even for a workman and his family, on
a Parliamentary train.

These vast and various changes were, of course,
spread over a considerable period: but the years between 1844 and 1848 brought them dramatically into
public notice, and saw the climax of a process begun
in the later 'twenties. Dickens had been prompt to
record in unobtrusive ways the earlier impact of railways on his world. One characteristic attitude found
expression in Mr. Weller's well-known outburst in
Master Humphrey's Clock against the 'unconstitootional
inwaser o' priwileges, . . . a nasty, wheezin', creakin',

---

[1] The peak year for the authorization of new lines by Parliament was 1846,
with 4,538 miles; and for the opening of new lines for traffic 1848, with 1,182 miles,
of which 604 had been authorized in 1845 and 403 in 1846. These figures are for
the whole of the United Kingdom. *Punch's Almanack* for 1846 is the only one
based entirely on a railway motif.

[2] It is hardly fanciful to associate the neater hedging and ditching of the middle
and later Victorian age with the necessary primness of railway works. More
scientific farming played its part; but there was also a new pride in neatness for its
own sake, which abolished the tangled hedgerows of Constable.

> . . . only ten or twelve
> Strokes of havoc unselve
> The sweet especial scene.

138

gaspin', puffin', bustin' monster, alvays out o' breath, vith a shiny green-and-gold back, like a unpleasant beetle in that 'ere gas magnifier'. Dickens also used the contrast between coach and train in the essay he wrote when giving up the editorship of *Bentley's Miscellany* in 1839, and was

> led insensibly into an anticipation of those days to-come when mail-coach guards shall no longer be judges of horse-flesh—when a mail-coach guard shall never even have seen a horse—when stations shall have superseded stables, and corn shall have given place to coke. 'In those dawning times,' thought I, 'exhibition rooms shall teem with portraits of Her Majesty's favourite engine, with boilers after Nature by future Landseers. . . .'[1]

It is interesting to find him so early (and in an essay mainly implying regret) taking it for granted even in a joke that railways would be everywhere victorious. Yet their comparatively small development combined with his own retrospective habit prevented mention of them in his major works. There is little railway in *Martin Chuzzlewit* (1843-5)[2]—there is a lot of comic and melodramatic business with coaches and chaises in the Pickwick style—but *Dombey*, written in the mania years, is full of it. It is first the ambition and then the life of fireman Toodle; it is the Car of Juggernaut as seen by *Punch*, with red eyes, bleared and dim, in the daylight, which licked up Carker's 'stream of life with its fiery heat, and cast his mutilated fragments in the air'. 'Express comes through at four, sir.—It don't stop.'

The first railway journey fully described in Dickens is that of Dombey and the Major on their way to

[1] In fact the railways caused a great increase in the number of horses, and a considerable increase, too, in horse-snobbery.

[2] It would be interesting to know how much truth there was in Mrs. Gamp's account of the many miscarriages caused by railway-travelling. It was believed that trains induced 'suicidal delirium' in nervous people.

Leamington. They started from Euston, where Hard-wick's gateway 'exhibiting the Grecian Doric upon a scale hitherto unattempted in modern times', not yet obscured by buildings round about it nor centralized by miles of solid building to the North, seemed indeed a monumental boundary to the town and an invitation to adventure beyond. To contemporaries the station was a matter for pride and curiosity:

> On passing within this gateway, we feel at once that as the mode of conveyance is different, so is the place. We are not within the narrow precincts of an inn-yard, jostled by porters and ostlers, and incommoded by luggage; everything is on a large scale. Yet one's old associations are disturbed by the sight of men in uniform keeping strict 'watch and ward', and by the necessary yet rigid exactness of all the arrangements. . . . 'First' and 'second' class passengers have their different entrances, and their separate booking desks; and on passing through the building have to produce their tickets as passports into the covered yard where the trains lie.[1]

Dombey travelled, as was then common, in his own carriage fastened to a flat truck. This comfortable independence of the gentry had its dangers no less than the inconveniences which Bagstock found; but it per-sisted for many years, and well on in the 'fifties Dr. Dionysius Lardner had to include among his rules for travellers: 'If you travel with your private carriage, do not sit in it on the railway. Take your place by preference in one of the regular railway carriages.'

Dombey and Bagstock apparently went right through to Birmingham (instead of leaving the train, as they might have done, at Rugby or Coventry), and drove down to Leamington from there. This made it possible for Dickens to extend his description of the travelling itself; and in doing so he established a standard, almost a formula, for such writing, which he followed several

[1] *The Penny Magazine*, Vol. VII, p. 329.

times later. The amount of observation he compresses into a few paragraphs is amazing. Some is of what we have all wondered at from childhood—the 'objects close at hand and almost in the grasp, ever flying from the traveller' contrasted with the slow movement of 'the deceitful distance'; the sensation of whirling backwards in a tunnel; the indifference of the train to weather; the drippings from a hydrant spout. The rhythm of the wheels he tries to catch in a rather blatant theme: 'Away, with a shriek, and a roar, and a rattle,' too often repeated; but in fact he catches it far more subtly and with brilliant success in the lists of things and scenes which the train passes; building on a fairly regular anapaestic base, he manages by many variations to convey those shifts and suspensions of beat caused in fact on a railway by passing points and crossings, by shorter lengths of rail and by a slight difference, perhaps, in the fixing of the chairs. The thing must be read aloud. Some of the description belongs to an early astonishment which we can never recapture; such, for instance, is the engineering-geological interest in cuttings—'through the chalk, through the mould, through the clay, through the rock'—which has so large a place in the popular railway literature of the time,[1] and focused in particular upon the works at Tring and Blisworth on the Birmingham line.

The method of the description as a whole is to combine the more immediate effects of speed upon the sight and hearing—'massive bridges crossing up above, fall like a beam of shadow an inch broad, upon the eye'—with a quick kaleidoscopic view of passing scenes,[2] which compel in their succession a number of social

---

[1] e.g. Lardner's books, George Measom's illustrated Guides, Smiles's *Life of George Stephenson*, and *Our Iron Roads*, by Frederick S. Williams.

[2] This is the method used also in *A Flight* (*Household Words*, Vol. III, August 30, 1851), which describes a journey by S.E.R. from London to Folkestone. The route was then: London Bridge, New Cross, Croydon, Reigate, Tunbridge, Ashford. The line through Sevenoaks was not built. And see *Our Mutual Friend*, Bk. IV, Chapter XI.

contrasts. Things seen from a carriage window enforced once more the gravity of the 'condition of England question'. The homes of the Two Nations might be seen as if from a single viewpoint, yet in their own settings. And on such a journey as this, which passed at least through the fringes of the Black Country, the southerner looked out with new surprise upon the industrial landscape.

Dickens repeated this effect of social contrast when he described in 1857 the journey of the two idle apprentices from London to Carlisle:[1]

> The pastoral country darkened, became coaly, became smoky, became infernal, got better, got worse, improved again, grew rugged, turned romantic; was a wood, a stream, a chain of hills, a gorge, a moor, a cathedral town, a fortified place, a waste. Now, miserable black dwellings, a black canal, and sick black towers of chimneys; now, a trim garden, where the flowers were bright and fair; now, a wilderness of hideous altars all a-blaze; now, the water meadows with their fairy rings; now, the mangy patch of unlet building ground outside the stagnant town, with the larger ring where the Circus was last week.

In the 'fifties the railway system was broadly as we know it now, and travellers were discovering the uncertain delights of cross-country journeys and of branch lines into remoter parts. Towards the end of Chapter III of the *Lazy Tour*, when the apprentices decide to stay at the Junction Station, the railways as a system come into their own,[2] and Dickens's prose shows once more its adaptability to new settings. We need not guess what their station was (it was too quiet for Crewe), but it had exactly the atmosphere of places like Trent

[1] *The Lazy Tour of Two Idle Apprentices*, Chapter I, *Household Words*, Vol. XVI, October 3, 1857.

[2] Dickens made a less benign and more commonplace comment on the system in *A Narrative of Extraordinary Suffering* (*Household Words*, Vol. III, p. 361, July 12, 1851), in which Mr. Lost goes off his head through trying to work out a journey from Bradshaw.

Valley and Bletchley, which the lack of planning in the 'forties first made notorious on the map:

> All manner of cross-lines of rails came zig-zagging into it, like a Congress of iron vipers; and, a little way out of it, a pointsman in an elevated signal-box was constantly going through the motions of drawing immense quantities of beer at a public-house bar. In one direction, confused perspectives of embankments and arches were to be seen from the platform; in the other, the rails soon disentangled themselves into two tracks, and shot away under a bridge, and curved round a corner. Sidings were there, in which empty luggage-vans and cattle-boxes often butted against each other as if they couldn't agree; and warehouses were there, in which great quantities of goods seemed to have taken the veil (of the consistency of tarpaulin), and to have retired from the world without any hope of getting back to it. Refreshment-rooms were there; one, for the hungry and thirsty Iron Locomotives where their coke and water were ready, and of good quality, for they were dangerous to play tricks with; the other, for the hungry and thirsty human Locomotives, who might take what they could get, and whose chief consolation was provided in the form of three terrific urns or vases of white metal, containing nothing, each forming a breastwork for a defiant and apparently much-injured woman.

Then come the startling alternations of boredom and hurry:

> The Station was either totally unconscious, or wildly raving. By day, in its unconscious state, it looked as if no life could come to it,—as if it were all rust, dust, and ashes—as if the last train for ever, had gone without issuing any Return-Tickets—as if the last Engine had uttered its last shriek and burst. One awkward shave of the air from the wooden razor, and everything changed. Tight office-doors flew open, panels yielded, books, newspapers, travelling-caps and wrappers broke out of brick walls, money chinked, conveyances oppressed by nightmares of luggage came careering into the yard, porters started up from secret places, ditto

the much-injured women, the shining bell, who lived in a little tray on stilts by himself, flew into a man's hand and clamoured violently. The pointsman aloft in the signal-box made the motions of drawing, with some difficulty, hogsheads of beer. Down Train! More beer. Up Train! More beer. Cross Junction Train! More beer. Cattle Train! More beer. Goods Train! Simmering, whistling, trembling, rumbling, thundering. Trains on the whole confusion of intersecting rails, crossing one another, bumping one another, hissing one another, backing to go forward, tearing into distance to come close. People frantic. Exiles seeking restoration to their native carriages, and banished to remoter climes. More beer and more bell. Then, in a minute, the Station relapsed into stupor as the stoker of the Cattle Train, the last to depart, went gliding out of it, wiping the long nose of his oil-can with a dirty pocket-handkerchief.

At night, when trains are signalled, the dead station breaks out suddenly with gas, and the advertisements jump to life on its walls:

By night, in its unconscious state, the station was not so much as visible. Something in the air, like an enterprising chemist's established in business on one of the boughs of Jack's beanstalk, was all that could be discerned of it under the stars. In a moment it would break out, a constellation of gas. In another moment, twenty rival chemists, on twenty rival beanstalks, came into existence. Then, the Furies would be seen, waving their lurid torches up and down the confused perspectives of embankments and arches —would be heard, too, wailing and shrieking. Then, the Station would be full of palpitating trains, as in the day; with the heightening difference that they were not so clearly seen as in the day, whereas the station walls, starting forward under the gas, like a hippopotamus's eyes, dazzled the human locomotives with the sauce-bottle, the cheap music, the bedstead, the distorted range of buildings where the patent safes are made, the gentleman in the rain with the registered umbrella, the lady returning from the ball with the registered respirator, and all their other embellishments.

It is painful to stop quoting: there follows a magnificent description of the frightened animals in cattle-trucks, and another of the man with a hammer tapping wheels. After such writing (and there is more, nearly as good, about Mugby Junction in the 'sixties) it is impossible to say, as Gissing said, that Dickens never described railways with the same vision, gusto, and enjoyment as he described coaches: he goes far beyond the making of common records. Though he is tainted with the prevailing facetiousness about refreshment-rooms and luggage and wrappers, the stand-bys of *Punch*, he uses it infinitely better than *Punch*. There is as much genuine humour in these descriptions of a station as in anything he ever wrote about the yard of the Saracen's Head or the Golden Cross. And in the last part of this passage he turns upon the railway the same imaginative eye as saw the London fogs and Cooling marshes.

But whereas the fogs and marshes have a direct emotional connexion with the stories in which they appear, these railway scenes, however brilliant, are rather episodes or interludes in stories on a quite different plane. Yet there is never the feeling, even in the *Lazy Tour*, that he puts in some railway stuff for the sake of up-to-date 'colour'. Indeed, it has more life and spontaneity than what surrounds it: there was never anything merely whimsical in his emotions about trains; they are closely based on physical experience. He had the railway mood spasmodically: he did not live and create in it, except perhaps in *Dombey*. But when the mood was on him his understanding of the sensual and social effects of the whole railway revolution was deeper and wider than that of his contemporaries.[1]

[1] As an editor Dickens gave the railways a lot of space. *Household Words* and *All the Year Round* are full of railway stories, railway verses, and articles on railway policy and pleasures. There are some obvious imitations of Dickens among them, but neither these nor things in quite different styles succeed, as his stories do, in being emotionally at home in the setting they have chosen. An article called *Poetry on the Railway* (*Household Words*, Vol. XI, p. 414, June 2, 1855) makes very clear the kind of difficulty that writers felt: for though it is mainly a facetious

The scenery and mood of *Dombey* belong to the
Railway Age and the London townscape, too, is transformed: it is in London that Dickens's pulse must be
taken. The very office of 'The Firm of Dombey and
Son, Wholesale, Retail, and for Exportation' has failed
to keep his attention; many details in it are certainly
described, but they are dead—hardly a reader would
remember them. All his passionate interest in office
furniture and routine, ledgers and rulers and ink, which
leaves a trail of immortal offices through others of his
books, has here declined into perfunctory humdrum.
The focus of his attention has shifted from the well-
known scenes of his youth to the new London of his
manhood. The focus is on Stuccovia, the suburbs, and
the terminus districts. The Dombey house 'between
Portland Place and Bryanston Square' is the first of a
series of dreary mansions continued in the houses of
Merdle and Boffin. The relevant business-men no
longer lived over their offices; and Dickens, moving
west, through Regency Bloomsbury towards Belgravia,

article, its tone seems rather assumed to hide a genuine attempt to argue against
the belief that the railways were 'at war with old poetic feeling', as Wordsworth
had found them in 1833. Wordsworth had held out the hope that they might
engender a new poetic feeling of their own; but when the writer of this article has
written with a good deal of sense of the excitements of going through a tunnel in
an open third-class carriage, he ultimately goes back to the Styx, Tartarus, Virgil,
and Dante; and he even compares the engine's whistle to the 'scream that they say
Catherine of Russia gave on her deathbed'. He wants to push the railways back
into terms of the old feeling, instead of adapting the feeling to them, and taking
its imagery from them.

In *All the Year Round* (Vol. XI, p. 180, April 2, 1864) there are some interesting
verses called *A Railway Reverie* which start with an honest and fairly successful
attempt to apply Tennysonian methods of description to mechanical things:

> The dry tense cords against the signal-post
> Rattle, like rigging of a wind-tossed ship;
> And, overhead, up staring at the sun,
> The scarlet target, duly split in half,
> Silently tells that soon the gliding train,
> Long-jointed, black, and winding, will glide in
> With clamp, and roar, and hiss, and shrieking scream. . . .

But the theme of the poem is the commonplace fancy that instead of facing physical
death and inevitable burial a man might get into a supernatural train at a natural
station and be carried off to vanishing-point—a mere piece of private, substitute
mythology.

was moving in his art towards the problem of boredom. How was dullness to be enforced without being dull? One of his answers is the beginning of Chapter XXI of *Little Dorrit*.

It has often been debated by Dickensians whether Dickens 'loved' London or not. An anonymous writer some years ago tried to answer part of this curious and complex question as follows:[1]

> If we are thinking of the real London, it is plain that such a thoroughly Philistine Radical as Dickens, who cared not twopence for history, who perceived chiefly the Tite Barnacles at St. Stephen's, 'wiglomeration' at Westminster, and the stench of rotting corpses in the City churches, was deprived of the most obvious reasons for loving it. No ancient city is a particularly lovable place to a keen reformer with a strong taste for police work. But the truth is probably that London got less and less lovable to him as he grew older, for it was continually losing the features he cared for most. Nooks of tranquillity; such naïve pleasures as circuses, cheap waxworks, and melodramas; tavern life and the leisure to enjoy it; racy and contrasting types; queer trades, quaint shops, and the suggestive melancholy of decay—these things were being pulverized by machinery. The London of *Our Mutual Friend* is grimmer and drabber than the London of *Pickwick*, and Dickens clearly enjoys it less.

But the effects of machinery were very various. The Thames steamboats, for instance, started in 1814, were intensely popular with the public of the 'thirties, and definitely belonged to the London of Dickens's youth. In the *Sketches* they are a normal instrument of pleasure, opening up a London which neither the travellers nor Dickens thought of as grim, drab, tranquil, or decaying. It is not impossible that but for the steamboats Dickens himself might never have begun to be interested in the waterside; and it is certain that their coming on the Thames was regarded by lower and middle class

[1] *Times Literary Supplement*, June 5, 1924, reviewing *The London of Charles Dickens*, by E. Beresford Chancellor.

Londoners as an extension of their resources in leisure. Even Ruth Pinch, who haunts most memories in Fountain Court, had 'never half so good a stroll as down among the steam-boats on a bright morning'; and Tom himself, straight from the peace of Wiltshire, found new delights for his wondering eyes in the turmoil at the starting of the 'Ankwerks package'. The London even of Dickens's retrospection was partly mechanized; and he enjoyed it.

Nor is regret the prominent tone of his many descriptions of changing London in *Dombey* and afterwards. The London of *Dombey* is being altered chiefly by the railways. It is the London of the 'forties, where Tennyson and Carlyle used to walk together at night, and Carlyle raved against the suburbs as a 'black jumble of black cottages where there used to be pleasant fields', and they would both agree that it was growing into 'a strange chaos of odds and ends, this London'.[1] Dickens did not rave; he observed the chaos in ways that implied his comment: here is his description of the ambiguous belt on the northern side, where he put the house of John and Harriet Carker:

> The second home is on the other side of London, near to where the busy great north road of bygone days is silent and almost deserted, except by wayfarers who toil along on foot. . . . The neighbourhood in which it stands has as little of the country to recommend it, as it has of the town. It is neither of the town nor country. The former, like the giant in his travelling boots, has made a stride and passed it, and has set his brick-and-mortar heel a long way in advance; but the intermediate space between the giant's feet, as yet, is only blighted country, and not town; and, here, among a few tall chimneys belching smoke all day and night, and among the brick-fields and the lanes where turf is cut, and where the fences tumble down, and where the dusty nettles grow, and where a scrap or two of hedge may yet be seen, and

[1] *Tennyson, A memoir*, by Hallam, Lord Tennyson, I, p. 267.

where the bird-catcher still comes occasionally, though he swears every time to come no more—this second home is to be found.   [Chapter XXXIII.]

And he notes the jerrybuilders' work as 'a disorderly crop of beginnings of mean houses, rising out of the rubbish, as if they had been unskilfully sown there'. A similar tract of muddled territory in the 'fifties or early 'sixties on the south side is described in *Our Mutual Friend*, Book II, Chapter I:

> The schools . . . were down in that district of the flat country tending to the Thames, where Kent and Surrey meet, and where the railways still bestride the market-gardens that will soon die under them. . . . They were in a neighbourhood which looked like a toy neighbourhood taken in blocks out of a box by a child of particularly incoherent mind, and set up anyhow; here, one side of a new street; there, a large solitary public-house facing nowhere; here, another unfinished street already in ruins; there, a church; here, an immense new warehouse; there, a dilapidated old country villa; then, a medley of black ditch, sparkling cucumber-frame, rank field, richly cultivated kitchen-garden, brick viaduct, arch-spanned canal, and disorder of frowsiness and fog. As if the child had given the table a kick and gone to sleep.

The counterparts of this creeping expansion across the fields are the sudden changes closer in, which are directly the railway's doing: within the short life of little Paul the whole Camden Town district was transformed:

> There was no such place as Staggs's Gardens. It had vanished from the earth. Where the old rotten summer-houses once had stood, palaces now reared their heads, and granite columns of gigantic girth opened a vista to the railway world beyond. The miserable waste ground, where the refuse matter had been heaped of yore, was swallowed up and gone; and in its frowsy stead were tiers of warehouses,

crammed with rich goods and costly merchandise. The old by-streets now swarmed with passengers and vehicles of every kind; the new streets that had stopped disheartened in the mud and waggon-ruts, formed towns within themselves, originating wholesome comforts and conveniences belonging to themselves, and never tried nor thought of until they sprung into existence. Bridges that had led to nothing, led to villas, gardens, churches, healthy public walks. The carcasses of houses, and beginnings of new thoroughfares, had started off upon the line at steam's own speed, and shot away into the country in a monster train.

[Chapter XV.]

It is interesting to compare this reformer's admiration for what had been done with the plain delight of the earlier description of Camden Town in Chapter VI; the district had then just been rent by the first shock of the railway earthquake which produced 'a hundred thousand shapes and substances of incompleteness, wildly mingled out of their places'. The contrast is not between anything old and interesting and beautiful with the prosaic new which has replaced it, but between the process of change and the achievement. The process truly fascinated Dickens, the achievement merely wins sober moral approval; his love of everything strange and confused had splendid scope in the odd lines and shapes and disorders, the disruption of the normal visual pattern, caused by large public works; even when 'Our School' had gone, fascination came before regret:

We went to look at it, only this last Midsummer, and found that the Railway had cut it up root and branch. A great trunk-line had swallowed the play-ground, sliced away the schoolroom, and pared off the corner of the house; which, thus curtailed of its proportions, presented itself, in a green stage of stucco, profilewise towards the road, like a forlorn flat-iron without a handle, standing on end.[1]

[1] *Household Words*, Saturday, October 11, 1851.

To the railways also must partly be attributed the greater uniformity of manners which becomes apparent in Dickens's later books. It was said as early as 1844:

> We cannot help noticing the visible, and in general beneficial, influence of railroad travelling upon public manners. . . . The bringing various ranks and classes of mankind into more familiar intercourse and better humour with each other—the emancipation of the fair sex, and particularly of the middle and higher classes, from the prohibition from travelling in public carriages, which with the majority was a prohibition from travelling at all—the opportunities, so frequently improved, of making agreeable acquaintances— the circulation, as it were, of the current coin of the intellect —and the general tone of mutual frankness and civility so observable in railroad travellers, and *so new in the English character*, are producing rapid and important effects—and it seems as if we might say of this new *art*—as of the old— 'Emollit mores, nec sinit esse feros'.[1]

Dr. Arnold remarked, as he watched a train on the Rugby line: 'I rejoice to see it, and think that feudality is gone for ever.'[2] But the mixing of the classes hardly extended to the poor: the third-class accommodation was scandalous, and the introduction of Parliamentary trains, intended to give the poor greater facilities, in fact gave statutory sanction to a social distinction which the companies had already established. It was regarded as a startling innovation when, as late as 1872, the Midland began to run third-class carriages on all trains. There is no description of a third-class journey in all Dickens: when his poor people travel by train, they do so generally in the company of 'their betters', who apparently pay the fares. The mixing of the classes was of the upper with the middle, and of the various sections of the middle class with each other: and this reflected the general process of readjustment that

---

[1] *Quarterly Review*, Vol. 74, pp. 250–1, footnote.
[2] Quoted by Mona Wilson, *Early Victorian England*, II, p. 291.

was taking place between *Pickwick* and *Our Mutual Friend*.[1]

A great deal has been written and said about Dickens as a writer for 'the people'. Yet his chief public was among the middle and lower-middle classes, rather than among the proletarian mass. His mood and idiom were those of the class from which he came, and his morality throve upon class distinctions even when it claimed to supersede them. He belonged to the generation which first used the phrase 'the great unwashed' and provided a Chadwick to scrub the people clean. His 'class' character was well described by *Blackwood's* in June 1855:

> We cannot but express our conviction that it is to the fact that he represents a class that he owes his speedy elevation to the top of the wave of popular favour. He is a man of very liberal sentiments—an assailer of constituted wrongs and authorities—one of the advocates in the plea of Poor *versus* Rich, to the progress of which he has lent no small aid in his day. But he is, notwithstanding, perhaps more distinctly than any other author of the time, a *class* writer, the historian and representative of one circle in the many ranks of our social scale. Despite their descents into the lowest class, and their occasional flights into the less familiar ground of fashion, it is the air and breath of middle-class respectability which fills the books of Mr. Dickens.

It should hardly be necessary to stress the substantial truth of this judgement; but Dickens has so often been claimed as popular in other senses—by Chesterton as if he were the leader of a kind of peasants' revolt in Bloomsbury; by Mr. Jackson as if his heart were really devoted to the uniting of the workers of the world—that some insistence on it here, in addition to what has already been implied in other chapters, must be forgiven.

[1] 'The peer face to face with the farmer and the merchant,' said Harriet Martineau, 'and the mechanic face to face with mountain and forest and sea': *History*, Bk. VI, Chapter XVII.

Many misunderstandings have been caused by the fact that Dickens himself so often and in so many voices proclaimed the gospel that class distinctions do not matter so much as common humanity, nor rank so much as virtue. In his speeches he loved to quote

> The rank is but the guinea stamp,
> The man's the gowd for a' that.

In one speech (1844) he quoted 'the words of a great living poet, who is one of us, and who uses his great gifts, as he holds them in trust, for the general welfare—

> Howe'er it be, it seems to me,
> 'Tis only noble to be good.
> True hearts are more than coronets,
> And simple faith than Norman blood.

But that he *could* make such quotations, as he did, to audiences of working men, without the slightest trace of self-consciousness or condescension, only shows the confidence he had in his own class position. In the same speech in which he made the Tennyson quotation he also said: 'Differences of wealth, of rank, of intellect, we know there must be, and we respect them.' Sentiments like that of Tennyson, so frequent in Victorian literature, have their origin more in the assertion by the bourgeois of his essential similarity to the aristocrat than in any levelling denial of all differences everywhere. The English aristocracy, for centuries recruited from the middle classes, was forced into still closer cultural and social contact with them in the generation after 1832: only then began those interminable controversies about what a gentleman is, and the countless jokes about snobs. Compared with Thackeray and most of the *Punch* circle, for instance, Dickens steered through these dangers handsomely.

The snob problem was not acute before the 'forties.

In Dickens's earlier books the strata of class are different from those of the later. Even those *Sketches* which turn on counter-jumping treat it rather as a legitimate and intelligible sport than as a social menace. Mr. Pickwick thought of himself as a gentleman, but he slides quite easily up and down a considerable distance on the social scale: he would gladly have met the Cheerybles, who did not think of themselves as gentlemen, on equal terms, without needing to exploit his benevolence. The important thing is that people like Pickwick, Mr. Garland, and the Cheerybles in the positively good camp, others like Nupkins, Slammer, and Benjamin Allen among the neutrals, though not without class-consciousness, are quite without class pedantry. The same is true of nearly all the characters in *Martin Chuzzlewit*, though they are mostly bourgeois.[1] The predominant class theme in these novels is benevolence towards the poor and the satirization, as in Miss Monflathers, of its opposite: class is treated more as a problem in morals than in manners. Only in *Nicholas Nickleby* among the early novels is the question of manners and style of life at all prominent: the heavy attack on the more bounderish symptoms of aristocracy is perhaps of less importance than the unfortunate-gentlewoman tone of Mrs. Nickleby and the acute sensibility of such people as Miss Knag and the Kenwigses to the trials and ambiguities of their social position: but even in these there is nothing that might not have been described in the eighteenth century.

The general vagueness about class distinctions in these books has sometimes been attributed to a supposed deficiency in young Dickens's knowledge of the world; but Dickens's 18 was most men's 25, and in his work in Doctors' Commons and Parliament and in

---

[1] An exception must be made of the incidental account of the 'lofty family' of the brass and copper founder in Chapter IX, which foreshadows later developments.

miscellaneous reporting all over the country he must have had unusually good opportunities of observing all the details of social difference; and *David Copperfield* is reason enough for supposing that he did observe them. But why were they not used till 1849–50? The answer seems to be that the social atmosphere of the 'forties led him to revise his pattern of interpretation; and that as the shifting and mingling of classes became more *apparent* in the habits of London society he was better able to understand the implications of what he had observed in earlier years. In his own work this shifting is first plain in *Dombey and Son*.

Dombey himself is the first full-length Dickens business-man to be solemnly self-conscious about his 'station and its duties', and a good deal of his pride is class-pride. 'I beg,' he says to Edith, 'that Mrs. Granger's very different experiences may now come to the instruction of Mrs. Dombey.' He plays his wealth against Granger's family and speaks of Edith's 'worldly advancement' in her second marriage. He differs from business-men like Pickwick, Brownlow, the Cheerybles, and the Chuzzlewits not only in living far more expensively, but in the importance he attaches to doing so. His father had probably been the first to break away from the Chuzzlewit set, and he is the first to aim at the Skewtons': but the only kind of conquest he recognizes is assimilation. Historically, he represents the process of taming the aristocrats till they are fit for bourgeois society: he is successful only through his daughter, which is as it should be. Dickens originally set himself in Dombey a problem in personal psychology: he did not make it very interesting; but in proportion as he failed to make convincing the workings of Dombey's mind he gave more attention to the money-class context in which they were expressed. The effectiveness of his later portraits of middle-class snobs —Merdles, Podsnaps, Veneerings, and the rest—is largely achieved by the deliberate identification of the whole personality with the context.

Dickens was attempting to define within the middle classes some such boundary as he had already accepted in the lower between the respectable and the low. In the last resort he shared Magwitch's belief that money and education can make a 'gentleman', that birth and tradition count for little or nothing in the formation of style. The final wonder of *Great Expectations* is that in spite of all Pip's neglect of Joe and coldness towards Biddy and all the remorse and self-recrimination that they caused him, he is made to appear at the end of it all a really better person than he was at the beginning. It is a remarkable achievement to have kept the reader's sympathy throughout a snob's progress. The book is the clearest artistic triumph of the Victorian bourgeoisie on its own special ground. The expectations lose their greatness, and Pip is saved from the grosser dangers of wealth; but by the end he has gained a wider and deeper knowledge of life, he is less rough, better spoken, better read, better mannered; he has friends as various as Herbert Pocket, Jaggers, and Wemmick; he has earned in his business abroad enough to pay his debts, he has become third partner in a firm that 'had a good name, and worked for its profits, and did very well'. Who is to say that these are not advantages? Certainly not Dickens. But he shirks the implications of the reconciliation with Joe and Biddy: there is one emotional scene with friendliness all round, which shows that in spite of his new accent and new manners Pip is the same decent little fellow after all: but what if he had had no Herbert to fall back on, and had been forced to build his fortunes again from scratch in the old village with Gargerys and Wopsles? Dickens does not face this: he takes Pip's new class position as established, and whisks him off to the East, where gentlemen grow like mushrooms. Yet we do not feel that this is artistically wrong, as the final marriage to Estella is wrong:[1] for the book is the sincere, uncritical expression of a time when the whole class-drift was upwards and there was no reason to suppose that it would ever stop being so. The social ideals of Pip and Magwitch differ only in taste. Though Pip has shuddered at the convict for being coarse and low, he consoles him on his death-bed with the very thought that first fired and then kept alive his own love for Estella: 'You had a child. . . . She is a lady and very beautiful.'

Here is the story allegorized by Mr. Jackson, writing as a Marxist:

> Self-satisfied, mid-Victorian, British society buoyed itself up with as great 'expectations' of future wealth and glory as did poor, deluded Pip. If it had but known, its means of ostentation came from a source (the labour of the depressed and exploited masses) to which it would have been as shocked to acknowledge indebtedness as Pip was to find he owed all his acquired gentility to the patronage of a transported felon. Magwitch differed little from the uncouth monster which respectable society envisaged to itself as the typical 'labouring man'. And in literal truth, good, respectable society owed as much to these working men, and was as little aware of it, as was Pip of the source of his advantages. And respectable society is as little grateful as Pip, whenever the truth is revealed.

This would be very plausible if only the rest of the class distinctions in the novel were what Mr. Jackson makes them out to be:

> Such class-antagonism as there is in *Great Expectations* is not that between aristocrats (as such) and common people, but that between, on the one side, the 'gentlemen' (who are for one reason or another either crazily vengeful or callously

---

[1] The ending was altered to suit Bulwer Lytton, but only 'from and after Pip's return to Joe's, and finding his little likeness there'. Pip's success abroad was thus in the original scheme (Forster, Bk. IX, Chapter III).

cold-hearted and corrupt) and with them their sycophants
and attendant slum-hooligans and on the other, the honest,
working section of the population.

Applied in detail this means Bentley Drummle, Com-
peyson, and Pumblechook on one side, with Joe, Biddy,
Matthew and Herbert Pocket, Jaggers, and Wemmick
all lumped together on the other. This is virtually to
say that in the end class distinctions are identical with
moral distinctions, without even being particularly nice
about morals; it is to ignore all the facts of class difference that Dickens was so subtly analysing. It is in
things like Estella's early treatment of Pip, Pip's first
weeks with Herbert, Jaggers's treatment of Estella's
mother, and the behaviour of Trabb's boy, that these
real differences are to be found.

Chesterton professed to find in Trabb's boy the last
word upon the triumphant revolutionary sarcasm of
the English democracy; you might almost as well find
the ultimate English democrat in old Orlick, the soured
'hand' turning to crime because of his inferior status,
whom Mr. Jackson just leaves as a 'blackguard'—a
man who in another novel might well have been the
leader of a no-Popery mob or of physical-force Chartists.
The assault of Trabb's boy, which brings Pip's class-
consciousness to a head, is more personal than political:
Dickens doesn't mean that good clothes are worse than
bad or that they are intrinsically funny and that the
class that wears them is doomed to die of jeers. Trabb's
boy was not among those who pointed at Stephen
Spender (*Poems*, 1937, p. 22):

> I feared the salt coarse pointing of those boys
> Who copied my lisp behind me on the road.
>
> They were lithe, they sprang out behind hedges
> Like dogs to bark at our world. They threw mud
> And I looked another way, pretending to smile.
> I longed to forgive them, yet they never smiled.

As things were he was a good pin to prick Pip's conceit; but if he himself had come into a fortune, he would have been just as nasty about it as Pip in his own way; and his way might have been worse.

Great Expectations is the perfect expression of a phase of English society: it is a statement, to be taken as it stands, of what money can do, good and bad; of how it can change and make distinctions of class; how it can pervert virtue, sweeten manners, open up new fields of enjoyment and suspicion. The mood of the book belongs not to the imaginary date of its plot, but to the time in which it was written; for the unquestioned assumptions that Pip can be transformed by money and the minor graces it can buy, and that the loss of one fortune can be repaired on the strength of incidental gains in voice and friends, were only possible in a country secure in its internal economy, with expanding markets abroad: this could hardly be said of England in the 'twenties and 'thirties.

Pip's acquired 'culture' was an entirely bourgeois thing: it came to little more than accent, table manners, and clothes. In these respects a country gentleman with an estate in a remoter part of England would probably have been, even at Queen Victoria's accession, more like the neighbouring farmers than like Mr. Dombey. The process of diffusing standard 'educated', London and Home Counties, speech as the norm expected of a gentleman was by no means complete: its rapid continuance through the Dickens period was an essential part of the increasing social uniformity between the middle and upper classes, helped on by the development of the 'public' schools.[1]

---

[1] It is interesting that there is no description of such a school anywhere in Dickens, though he described so many different kinds of private school, and sent his own sons to Eton. The extension of the term 'public school' to an increasing number of boarding schools was a process of the 'forties. (See, for instance, McCulloch's *Account of the British Empire*, 3rd. ed., 1847, Vol. II, p. 329.) It was, of course, the most influential expression of the 'gentleman' idea.

We are told that Pip 'read' a great deal, and that he enjoyed it; but we do not know what he read, or how it affected his mind, or what kind of pleasures he got from it. He knew enough about Shakespeare and acting to realize that Mr. Wopsle turned Waldengarver was ridiculous; but what other delights he found in theatre-going in his prosperous days we are left to judge for ourselves; painting and music certainly had no large part in his life. People like Pip, Herbert Pocket, and Traddles have no culture but domestic comfort and moral decency. They are sensitive, lovable, and intelligent, but their normal activities are entirely limited to a profession and a fireside. When one of their kind extends his activities beyond this range it is in the direction of 'social work', and even that is likely to be governed by his profession, as Allan Woodcourt is a good doctor, and Mr. Milvey a good parson. David Copperfield's other activity is to write novels like *Great Expectations* and *David Copperfield*: so we come full circle.

David, of course, gives the clearest view of Dickens's social position, and it is very clear indeed. The shame and horror of manual work which runs through Chapter XI was even something less than Dickens confessed to Forster he had felt himself:

I became, at ten years old, a little labouring hind in the service of Murdstone and Grinby. . . . There were three or four of us, counting me. . . . No words can express the secret agony of my soul as I sunk into this companionship. . . . I worked from morning until night, with common men and boys, a shabby child. . . . I might easily have been, for any care that was taken of me, a little robber or a little vagabond. . . . That I suffered in secret, and that I suffered exquisitely, no one ever knew but I. . . . But I kept my own counsel, and I did my work. I knew from the first, that, if I could not do my work as well as any of the rest, I could not hold myself above slight and contempt. I soon became at least as expeditious and as skilful as either of the other boys. Though perfectly familiar with them, my conduct and manner were different enough from theirs to place a space between us. They and the men generally spoke of me as 'the little gent', or 'the young Suffolker'. . . . Mealy Potatoes uprose once, and rebelled against my being so distinguished; but Mick Walker settled him in no time.

These sentences are scattered over ten pages or so; but bringing them together in this way causes no distortion of emphasis. The emphasis is equally clear in David's relations with the Peggottys: for all his friendliness he is never anything but 'Mas'r Davy'. The friendliness exists not so much in spite of class barriers as because it derives its peculiar quality from crossing, without ignoring, them.

The class problem obviously becomes most acute when sexual love attempts to cross the boundaries. The calf-love of Kit for Miss Nell, resolved by death, is nothing beside the love of Gill Davis, in *The Perils of Certain English Prisoners*[1] for Miss Maryon:

> I well knew what an immense and hopeless distance there was between me and Miss Maryon; I well knew that I was no fitter company for her than I was for the angels; I well knew that she was as high above my reach as the sky over my head; and yet I loved her. What put it in my low heart to be so daring . . . I am unable to say; still, the suffering to me was just as great as if I had been a gentleman. I suffered agony—agony. I suffered hard, and I suffered long.

'Her poor, old, faithful, humble soldier' ends, unmarried, as a kind of domestic pensioner to the lady when she has long been the wife of Admiral Sir George Carton, Baronet.

But the typical situation is when the social position of the sexes is reversed. Dickens twice treated at length

---

[1] Christmas Story, 1857, *Household Words*, Vol. XVI. The first chapter and the third, from which this extract comes, were by Dickens.

the theme of the gentleman falling for the common girl, in *David Copperfield* and *Our Mutual Friend*; he skirmished round it a third time in *Little Dorrit*. Steerforth's seduction of Emily is prepared for by his slick dictum about the lower classes:

> They are not to be expected to be as sensitive as we are. Their delicacy is not to be shocked, or hurt very easily. They are wonderfully virtuous, I dare say. Some people contend for that, at least; and I am sure I don't want to contradict them. But they have not very fine natures, and they may be thankful that, like their coarse, rough skins, they are not easily wounded. [Chapter XX.]

The contempt of the Steerforth group for the Peggotty group is thrown into melodramatic relief in Chapter XXXII when David takes Mr. Peggotty to the Steerforth house. The lower classes are there plainly shown to be emotionally sensitive as well as virtuous; but Peggotty's first and sincere intention is to get Emily married to a man he thinks a scoundrel; his prepared answers to Mrs. Steerforth's objections are 'Raise her up' and 'Teach her better'. Emily is meanwhile justifying his faith in her by chatting colloquially to boatmen's children on the Italian shore. 'The young woman,' said Littimer, 'was very improvable, and spoke the languages; and wouldn't have been known for the same country person.' Everything, in fact, shows Emily worthy to become the lady she hoped to be. Even Pamela only did better in being more cunning.

The likeness to Pamela is closer in Lizzie Hexham, who enhances her attractiveness and her virtue by running away: but Eugene Wrayburn is more interesting and complex than Steerforth. In place of the glamour of school heroics there is the glamour of parasitic culture. It needs assault, battery, and all but drowning to bring him to the point of proposing marriage: Lizzie only gets a rather damaged gentleman, but even he is a prize. It is impossible not to take the voice of Twemlow, in the last chapter of *Our Mutual Friend,* as the voice of Dickens:

> If this gentleman's feelings of gratitude, of respect, of admiration, induced him (as I presume they did) to marry this lady . . . I think he is the greater gentleman for the action, and makes her the greater lady. I beg to say that when I use the word gentleman, I use it in the sense in which the degree may be attained by any man.

But the application is solely to Eugene: and how can any action of his make a 'greater lady' of a girl whose moral superiority to him has been hammered in with such unremitting emphasis, except on the assumption that she gains in status by becoming his wife?

Two things are interesting in this speech: its obvious sincerity and its obvious sophistry. Twemlow's ingenious phrasing very imperfectly conceals a sort of satisfaction in the fact that Eugene is really doing a very generous thing in marrying Lizzie, and that she is doing very well for herself by marrying him. This satisfaction is based on the acceptance of existing class distinctions in general, while allowing that in particular cases the right thing is to cross them: they are not ignored as irrelevant, otherwise all the relish in the crossing would be lost. It was essential to the strength of a large bourgeoisie like the English to admit the principle of recruitment from below as a counterpart to the claim to provide recruits for the aristocracy; but such recruitment had to be controlled by a certain standard of taste and morals: money alone was not enough.

A great part of Dickens's later social satire is directed against people who believe that genteel territory can be entered with no passport but wealth; it is a common enough theme, but it was of peculiar importance in the mid-Victorian Age, and Dickens's attitude to it can only be understood by looking at economic developments from the 'forties to the 'seventies. In a previous chapter we saw the immense importance he attached to money in everything he wrote, and noted then that in the earlier novels finance is very individualistic, and that the typical bad rich man is the usurer. Beneath his hatred of people like Ralph Nickleby, Gride, and Quilp is the ancient moral feeling that usury is wrong because it enables people to make money without having to work for it, and that the power conferred by money earned in this way is the more hateful for its illegitimacy. Dickens was very careful, even when he was detaching his benevolent rich men from the immediate economic struggle, to insist that they *had*, at least in the past, worked for what they spent so generously. It is immaterial that he did so in an unconvincing way: the important thing is that people like the Cheerybles and Pickwick represent a stage of capitalist development in which the capitalist is normally an active member of a fairly small firm—that is also what Nicholas, Pip, and Arthur Clennam become— a man whose work bears a relation to his income similar to that of professional people to theirs. Such people as this (together with the professionals) were the basis of the 'respectable' middle class that Dickens represented.

The speculating manias of 1825–6 and 1837 on the whole endorsed the morality behind this view of society, because they were followed by economic collapse, meaning loss and ruin for people like Mr. Nickleby. The railway boom of 1845–6 meant ruin, too, for many, but it meant success for others, and by establishing the joint-stock company in a number of enormous undertakings pointed the way to the later developments of investing. By an Act of 1844 all joint-stock companies had to be registered with an official registrar, and this helped to restrain the activities of such people as Montague Tigg: and the principle of limited liability was first recognized in the legislation of 1855-6. The years between 1850 and 1866 were marked by a great increase in the number of small investors, and the later part of the period saw the growth of the system of finance companies, of which the most famous was the firm of Overend and Gurney.

These changes are clearly reflected in Dickens's work. With *Dombey and Son* the perpetual interest in money enters on a new phase. The famous dialogue between Paul and his father beginning 'Papa! what's money?' has often been quoted to show how Dickens rose above sordid and worldly things: but there is a special interest in the answer Mr. Dombey might have given, but did not:

> Mr. Dombey was in a difficulty. He would have liked to give him some explanation involving the terms circulating-medium, currency, depreciation of currency, paper, bullion, rates of exchange, value of precious metals in the market, and so forth; but looking down at the little chair, and seeing what a long way down it was, he answered: 'Gold, and silver, and copper. Guineas, shillings, half-pence. You know what they are?' [Chapter VIII.]

In the earlier novels finance is very individualistic; from *Dombey* onwards, though the interest in money's personal power still continues, and is indeed a main theme of *Great Expectations*, money as a system is even more important. The fortunes of nearly everybody in *Little Dorrit* and *Our Mutual Friend* hang on the big capitalists. Dickens does not make the mysteries of their finance clear, and does not mean to.

> Mr. Merdle was immensely rich; a man of prodigious enterprise; a Midas without the ears, who turned all he touched to gold. He was in everything good, from banking to building. He was in Parliament, of course. He was in the City, necessarily. He was Chairman of this, Trustee of that, President of the other. The weightiest of men had said

to projectors, 'Now, what name have you got? Have you got Merdle?' And, the reply being in the negative, had said, 'Then I won't look at you.'

[*Little Dorrit*, Chapter XXI.]

His power over people is greater in the long run because it is indirect; but it is not a terrifying power like Quilp's—he does not bully people with investments—for the success of Merdle is the success of all; so far his dupes, and the system they all belong to, are to blame. The villain is 'the City'. Dickens cannot build up Merdle as a villain; in fact he makes him rather attractive, shuffling and slinking through the pointless grandeur, frightened of the butler he has hired and the bosom he has bought. His imitation of a Roman death brings ruin to thousands whose names he never even knew; but their anger turns as much against those who, by their trust and avarice, established his credit, as against him. According to the imaginary date of the book the Merdle crash is part of the financial collapse of 1825–6; but the extent of Merdle's operations, the number of small investors involved in them, and the position they give him in society belong entirely to the 'fifties. It is noticeable too that the part played by Mr. Meagles in this financial atmosphere is muted and cautious; he still represents the old idea of generous benevolence, but he has no longer the same freedom, scope, and innocence of the Christmassy people. He is relatively powerless in circumstances which can lure even the staid Arthur Clennam into speculation.

The treatment of money and investment is even broader and more scathing in *Our Mutual Friend*. To begin with, the great Harmon fortune, on which everything turns, has not been made from banking or building, nor from railways even, but from dust. Dickens had evidently had these great suburban dust-heaps in mind for at least fourteen years: a sort of story-article on them had appeared in *Household Words* on July 13, 1850. Their chief value was then said to be in the ashes, which were used for brick-making, while the soot section of the heap was good for manure.

> Their worth, however, varies not only with their magnitude . . . but with the demand. About the year 1820, the Marylebone Dust-heap produced between four thousand and five thousand pounds. In 1832, St. George's paid Mr. Stapleton five hundred pounds a year, not to leave the Heap standing, but to carry it away. Of course he was only too glad to be paid highly for selling his dust.

They also had other more accidental sources of value; gold and silver articles were sometimes found in them, and in one heap in 1847 a banker's cheque for a considerable amount turned up. But this article does not deal with the really sinister question that must be asked about the Harmon mounds. One of the main jobs of a dust-contractor in Early Victorian London was to collect the contents of the privies and the piles of mixed dung and ashes which were made in the poorer streets; and the term 'dust' was often used as a euphemism for decaying human excrement, which was exceedingly valuable as a fertilizer. Some contemporary readers at least must have thought of the mounds as being partly composed of such stuff; and then the idea of Silas Wegg prodding them with his wooden leg becomes almost intolerable.

By choosing such a source for the money on which his whole story was to depend and adding a jumble of intricate wills (though he protested that such things were quite true to life), Dickens makes plain enough that the whole business of earning money or inheriting it can be detached altogether from any reasonable scheme of life. Collecting dirt is not a kind of work that deserves munificent rewards. Apart from the Harmon fortune the financial system is more explicitly condemned: the Podsnaps, Veneerings, and Lammles live in a world in which investment has taken the place of work:

> As is well known to the wise in their generation, traffic in Shares is the one thing to have to do with in this world. Have no antecedents, no established character, no cultivation, no ideas, no manners; have Shares. Have Shares enough to be on Boards of Direction in capital letters, oscillate on mysterious business between London and Paris, and be great. Where does he come from? Shares. Where is he going to? Shares. What are his tastes? Shares. Has he any principles? Shares. What squeezes him into Parliament? Shares. Perhaps he never of himself achieved success in anything, never originated anything, never produced anything! Sufficient answer to all; Shares. O mighty Shares! To set those blaring images so high, and to cause us smaller vermin, as under the influence of henbane or opium, to cry out night and day, 'Relieve us of our money, scatter it for us, buy us and sell us, ruin us, only we beseech ye take rank among the powers of the earth, and fatten on us!'
>
> [*Our Mutual Friend*, Book I, Chapter X.]

This paragraph would have had special force in the years just before the crisis of 1866, which saw the failure of Overend and Gurney and the collapse of many companies that had come into existence in the past ten years.

The increase of the rentier class and of entirely 'new' people like the Veneerings seriously disturbed Dickens's idea of the extent to which good individuals could redress the evils of social inequality. It is often said that because Boffin appears in *Our Mutual Friend* Dickens never really abandoned the optimistic view that if you had enough Cheerybles all would be well; but Boffin's whole behaviour is so wildly different from that of the earlier benevolent people that he seems almost to be a critical caricature of them. To begin with (for his wife's sake, so he says), he makes concessions to fashion the Cheerybles never dreamed of making, and goes in for all the business of carriages and parties as strong as the Veneerings themselves. Even apart from his pretended miserhood he behaves to Silas Wegg rather like mistresses who leave half-crowns in corners hoping the servants will steal them; and the episode of the miserhood is so convincingly done that one is tempted to wonder whether Dickens did not mean it to be genuine and only changed his mind towards the end. But even if he meant it to be a deception all along, it shows the need he felt for some very elaborate artifice to get the mercenary ideas out of Bella's head in the kind of society she was living in; everything is corrupted and distorted by money, and even some of Boffin's benevolent schemes are thwarted. Roughly one may say that he belongs to the Cheeryble group; Sloppy is his Smike, the Rev. Frank his Trimmers: but he is operating against greater obstacles, with less confidence and less success. For Dickens felt that his old solution did not so surely apply in high mid-Victorian prosperity, when the simpler social categories within which he had worked had broken down.

CHAPTER VII

POLITICS

```
                                                          night
_____
                                            to
Sir, when I came do              this house
_____
                    o
_____
                        o
_____
                    wn to
_____
                                                          ters
                                        Minis
_____
                                    ty's
I found Her                      jes
_____

_____

_____
                    Ma
```

From Dickens's *A Few Conventionalities*, 1851

THE most instructive political characteristic of the years from 1825 to 1845 is the growth and influence of the scheme of opinion which we call Radicalism. There are several species of creeds which are comprehended under this generic name, but they all evince a marked reaction against the worship of the English Constitution and the affection for the English *status quo*, which were then the established creed and sentiment. All Radicals are Anti-Eldonites. This is equally true of the Benthamite or philosophical radicalism of the early period, and the Manchester, or 'definite-grievance radicalism', among the last vestiges of which we are now living. Mr. Dickens represents a species different from either. His is what we may call the 'sentimental radicalism'; and if we recur to the history of the time, we shall find that there would not originally have been any opprobrium attaching to such a name.

This paragraph is from Bagehot's essay of 1858 already quoted in the chapter on 'Benevolence'; and it is in the light of that chapter that Dickens's political writing must be discussed: for it is not always possible to make a clear distinction between Charity and Politics in Victorian Social history; voluntary associations of many kinds were often instrumental, through such people as Fowell Buxton, Mrs. Chisholm, and Ashley, in widening the sphere of Government against the drift of current political thought. The technique of legislation being far more flexible than at the present day, it was possible for private members to carry reforms from philanthropic motives without raising strictly political issues. The voting on some of the most significant Victorian Acts of Parliament ignored all recognized party distinctions. So the social opinions of ordinary men could not be divided into political and non-political: the obscure work of a local Benevolent Society might suddenly become matter of politics tomorrow. Personal cleanliness became Public Health: even a place so private as the grave could be the subject of unexpected official inquiry.

It means very little that Dickens called himself a Radical or that Bagehot called him one, if the word must be tied down to some exact significance. He certainly was not a Radical as Henry Hunt or Bamford were Radicals, nor as the Chartists or the men of the *Westminster Review*. He was not of those radicals whose principles, of which he heard as a boy, were that the Prince Regent wore stays, that nobody had a right to any salary, and that the army and navy ought to be put down. He was not one of Disraeli's 'low rads'. The noun 'radical' was still fairly new in his time, and perhaps by so often arrogating it to himself he helped to extend its application to cover almost any person whose sympathies, whenever occasion offered, were with the under-dog. It came to lose its connexion with the idea of going to the root of the matter. And even if the root of the matter did truly lie in the simple sentiment of human benevolence, there still remained the problem of how this sentiment was to find expression in the wider forms of social and national life. A person of Dickens's temper could not ignore politics in any case; and his own early life was such that politics in the narrowest technical sense remained a permanent irritant that would not give him peace.

The epigrammatic symbol of political faith to which he committed himself near the end of his life has annoyed the more sophisticated commentators and provoked the more simple to ecstasies at its profundity: its value, even if it be a truism, can be best assessed from the whole context, including the explanation that Dickens himself gave. At the Birmingham and Midland Institute on September 27, 1869, replying to a vote of thanks in a short additional speech, he used these words:

> I will now discharge my conscience of my political creed, which is contained in two articles, and has no reference to any party or persons. My faith in the people governing is, on the whole, infinitesimal; my faith in the People governed is, on the whole, illimitable.

By a strange subtlety of interpretation this dictum was taken by some people at the time, and by others more seriously since, to imply some anti-democratic belief; and even those who interpret it democratically twist it about to suit various purposes of their own. Dickens himself was back in Birmingham the next January, and felt that he ought to explain what he meant:

> When I was here last autumn I made, in reference to some remarks of your respected member, Mr. Dixon, a short confession of my political faith—or perhaps I should better

say want of faith. It imported that I have very little confidence in the people who govern us—please to observe
'people' there will be with a small 'p'—but that I have great
confidence in the People whom they govern; please to
observe 'people' there with a large 'P'. This was shortly
and elliptically stated, and was with no evil intention, I am
absolutely sure, in some quarters inversely explained. Perhaps . . . I do not sufficiently bear in mind Hamlet's caution
to speak by the card lest equivocation should undo me.

Now I complain of nobody; but simply in order that there
may be no mistake as to what I did mean, and as to what
I do mean, I will re-state my meaning, and I will do so in
the words of a great thinker, a great writer, and a great
scholar, whose death, unfortunately for mankind, cut short
his *History of Civilization in England*: 'They may talk as they
will about reforms which Government has introduced and
improvements to be expected from legislation, but whoever
will take a wider and more commanding view of human
affairs, will soon discover that such hopes are chimerical.
They will learn that lawgivers are nearly always the ob-
structors of society instead of its helpers, and that in the
extremely few cases where their measures have turned out
well, their success has been owing to the fact that, contrary
to their usual custom, they have implicitly obeyed the spirit
of their time, and have been—as they always should be—the
mere servants of the people, to whose wishes they are bound
to give a public and legal sanction.'

This quotation from Buckle is one of the most interesting episodes in the slight history of Dickens's
opinions; for the *History of Civilization* brought together
so many strands of the 'advanced' thought of the Early
Victorian Age—the belief in progress, the emphasis on
statistics, the hatred of superstition, the nationalism,
the interest in the physical influences on character—
that it is strange to find Dickens quoting it with such
approval. From one point of view Buckle's book can
be seen as an attempt to erect the doctrine of *laissez-
faire* into a philosophy of history, and to defend

civilized society as a state of benevolent and genial anarchy. The passage which Dickens quotes from the chapter on the Condition of Scotland in the Seventeenth and Eighteenth Centuries should be read together with that on the Influence exercised by Religion, Literature and Government;[1] for there Buckle develops the idea of the obstructiveness of legislation:

> Every great reform which has been effected has consisted, not in doing something new, but in undoing something old. . . . The whole scope and tendency of modern legislation is, to restore things to that natural channel from which the ignorance of preceding legislation has driven them. This is one of the great works of the present age; and if legislators do it well, they will deserve the gratitude of mankind. But though we may thus be grateful to individual lawgivers, we owe no thanks to lawgivers considered as a class. For since the most valuable improvements in legislation are those which subvert preceding legislation, it is clear that the balance of good cannot be on their side.

The two chief examples given in support of this thesis are the emancipation of the Catholics and the Repeal of the Corn Laws; and Buckle carries his argument so far as to say that the commercial reforms which had distinguished England during the last twenty years had consisted solely in undoing mischievous and intrusive legislation.

It is obviously not possible to attribute all these ideas to Dickens, but they indicate fairly the climate in which his 'political creed' was formulated, and have an important bearing on his attitude to specific pieces of legislation and to the Legislature itself. A great deal of the legislation that he is known to have approved in his lifetime was of the negative, destructive kind spoken of by Buckle. *The Daily News* was founded mainly to advocate the repeal of the Corn Laws, and

[1] See especially pp. 156–7 in J. M. Robertson's ed. (Routledge, N.D.).

during the short period of Dickens's editorship an immense proportion of its space was given to that one subject. In his miscellaneous journalism he supported such various things as the repeal of the window-tax; of the stamp-duties on newspapers, periodicals, and paper; of the laws allowing imprisonment for debt— and so on. And a great part of his advocacy of wider law reform was in the same spirit and according to the opinion of his time. He was often more concerned to simplify the procedure of the law, which had become fantastically intricate and expensive by centuries of accumulation, than to put forward any new legal principles. His aim was that every citizen should be able to get the justice that the law theoretically recognized by the simplest possible route. This is true both of his grand attacks on the soul-destroying delays of the Court of Chancery and of such comparatively minor things as the amendment of the Patent Law[1] and the Law of Divorce. He also opposed various attempts, such as the Sunday Observance Bill, to impose new restrictions on popular liberty. But it is quite impossible, as we shall see, to saddle Dickens with the opinion that *the only* beneficial legislation of the time was of this negative, repealing kind: he exemplifies very clearly the dilemma between *laissez-faire* and interference.

But there is another, antecedent, dilemma in Buckle's position, which is very relevant. 'Lawgivers', as a class, are said to legislate generally against the interests of society and against the spirit of their time: this implies that more often than not public opinion has no

---

[1] Daniel Doyce's troubles in *Little Dorrit* were rather out of date when they were published. Dickens's article *A Poor Man's Tale of a Patent* was directed against the worst anomalies which were done away with by the Patent Law Amendment Act of 1852. By that Act all Patent business was conducted in one office, costs were reduced, and the rules about specifications were revised: there was no real change in principle. See David Fulton: *Law of Patents and Designs*, 4th ed., pp. 11–12.

influence on legislation: but Buckle goes on to say that the lawgivers' only successful measures are those in which they have implicitly obeyed the spirit of their time: and this implies that on some crucial occasions public opinion is the determining factor. But if public opinion can sometimes assert itself in this way, how does it happen that the lawgivers can predominantly legislate against it? This is the problem behind Dickens's antithesis between the 'people governing' and the 'People governed'. It is useless to look in his work for any theoretical answer to it: such answer as he gives must be found in his practical attitude to particular acts of English government.

Dickens's Parliamentary satire plays rather monotonously on the one idea that even after the Reform Bill of '32, M.P.s were still largely drawn from a few families of an obsolete ruling class—Coodle, Doodle, and Sir Leicester, Buckle obstructionists—or from classes likely to be corrupted by the prevailing Parliamentary style—people like Merdle and Veneering. Neither in the novels nor in the journalism does he show any interest in the complex interaction of personalities on which the history of Victorian Parliamentary government so much depends; even when actual politicians[1] are introduced in thin disguise they are often indistinguishable from the imagined types; his politicians are mere mouthpieces of formulae and pullers of strings. His mistrust of Parliamentary institutions as a whole is a consequence of this sweeping condemnation of the people who run them:

> I do not remember having ever fainted away, or having even been moved to tears of joyful pride, at sight of any legislative body. I have borne the House of Commons like a man, and have yielded to no weakness, but slumber, in the House of Lords. I have seen elections for borough and county, and have never been impelled (no matter which

[1] e.g. in *The Thousand and One Humbugs.* 1855.

176

party won) to damage my hat by throwing it up into the air in triumph, or to crack my voice by shouting forth any reference to our Glorious Constitution, to the noble purity of our independent voters, or, the unimpeachable integrity of our independent members.[1]

And the same attitude colours his political approach to labour problems:

I greatly fear that until governments are honest, and Parliaments pure, and great men less considered, and small men more so, it is almost a cruelty to limit, even the dreadful hours and wages of Labor which at this time prevail. . . . The necessity of a mighty change, I clearly see. . . .[2]

It is interesting in the light of these two quotations to realize that, not long before, Dickens had himself seriously considered the possibility of entering Parliament. In reply to an invitation to stand as a candidate for Reading[3] he said that he could not afford the expense of a contested election, and that even if he were elected his duties in the House would take time that would mean great financial sacrifices. He seems, however, to suggest that the Government (i.e. Melbourne's second administration) would almost certainly be willing to pay his election expenses. 'But I cannot satisfy myself,' he added, 'that to enter Parliament in such circumstances would enable me to pursue that honourable independence without which I could neither preserve my own respect nor that of my constituents.' In later years, when asked to stand for Parliament, his refusals were categorical and severe: once he said: 'I believe that no consideration would induce me to become a member of that extraordinary assembly.' At another time: 'It appears to me that the House of Commons and Parliament altogether is become just

[1] *American Notes*, Chapter VIII. 1842.
[2] Letter to Southwood Smith, February 1, 1843.
[3] Letters to G. Lovejoy, May 31 and June 10, 1841.

the dreariest failure and nuisance that ever bothered this much-bothered world.'

Attempts have sometimes been made to find in his 1842 visit to America the great turning-point in his political opinions, the beginning of disillusionment with representative government and all popular institutions. It is true that to some English radicals even in the 'forties America appeared as the Holy Land of Liberty; but there is little evidence that it appeared so to Dickens before he went there; he went in a mood of high personal excitement and curiosity, mainly induced by his own reputation, and the first and greatest disillusionment was over the question of Copyright. There is enough in his writing before 1842 to show the way his political sympathies were shaping. *A Parliamentary Sketch*, the Eatanswill election, and the Gregsbury episode in *Nicholas Nickleby* all fully bear out what he said after seeing the American House of Representatives in action over a very stormy period; and even then he thought fit to add that farmyard imitations had not as yet been imported from the Parliament of the United Kingdom. His experience in both countries was leading him to the conclusion that elected assemblies of those kinds were inadequate as legislatures and also inadequate as a means of bringing public opinion to bear on the executive. So far as England was concerned he saw almost from his boyhood that the imperfections of Parliament were largely caused by the initial corruption of its members through the very process of election. Influence, whether financial or social, counted for more than merit; the influence was more often than not corruptly exercised; and even when technical corruption did not enter in, the far more subtle corruption of electioneering promises and party propaganda undermined the morale of an M.P. from the start. Nearly all his attacks on Parliament can be reduced to this suspicion of the personal sincerity and independence of its members.

Dickens might have sided with the Chartists. They believed that Universal Manhood suffrage—combined with the secret ballot and a limitation of each Parliament's life, and various other restrictions on the influence of property in elections—would produce a free, independent assembly which honestly represented the people as a whole. But two things prevented Dickens's accepting this position—his horror of 'the mob' and (what was closely allied with it) his belief in the infallible virtues of education. In the first of these he was deeply influenced by the events of his time, and was more ready to follow a middle-class scare than to examine the causes of it. There is nothing more surprising in all his work than the sudden irruption of his fears of Chartism into *The Old Curiosity Shop*. Little Nell and her grandfather come in their aimless wanderings to the industrial midlands and Dickens then properly records the ordinary Southerner's surprise at what they see, but imposed upon it is the following paragraph:

But, night-time in this dreadful spot!—night, when the smoke was changed to fire; when every chimney spirted up its flame; and places, that had been dark vaults all day, now shone red-hot, with figures moving to and fro within their blazing jaws, and calling to one another with hoarse cries— night, when the noise of every strange machine was aggravated by the darkness; when the people near them looked wilder and more savage; when bands of unemployed labourers paraded the roads, or clustered by torch-light round their leaders, who told them, in stern language, of their wrongs, and urged them on to frightful cries and threats; when maddened men, armed with sword and firebrand, spurning the tears and prayers of women who would restrain them, rushed forth on errands of terror and destruction, to work no ruin half so surely as their own—night, when carts came

179

rumbling by, filled with rude coffins (for contagious disease
and death had been busy with the living crops); when
orphans cried, and distracted women shrieked and followed
in their wake—night, when some called for bread, and some
for drink to drown their cares, and some with tears, and some
with staggering feet, and some with bloodshot eyes, went
brooding home—night, which, unlike the night that Heaven
sends on earth, brought with it no peace, nor quiet, nor
signs of blessed sleep—who shall tell the terrors of the night
to the young wandering child! [Chapter XLV.]

This piece of metrical excitement was chosen to be
illustrated by Hablot Browne. He showed the front
of a mob armed with guns, pistols, knives, scythes,
pikes, and flaming torches, led on under a banner
bearing skull and cross-bones to pillage the tall-
chimneyed town that fills the background. Neither
the description nor the picture has anything whatever
to do with Little Nell. The people of this crowd
were not Chartists, but they were typical of what a
great part of the industrial workers were thought to
be in the Chartist period, a barbarous and awful horde.
The theme of mob-violence was so much in Dickens's
mind that his next novel centred on the Gordon Riots,
which he sees less as something that had in fact
happened sixty years before than as something that
might happen in 1840; and his horrible imaginings
stream on in an almost hysterical rhythm.

It is not necessary to infer that these descriptions
grow from the purely economic fear avowed by
Macaulay in his speech against the Chartists; they
grow rather from a psychological pacifism based on
an introspective knowledge of the hidden depths of
bestiality in every man. Politics is in the last resort
a question of power, and in the black years from
1839–42 Dickens made it clear enough that, as things
were, he did not want power to go by mere majority.
But power as it then existed by law established was

little better, and was indeed partly a cause of the anarchic looting that threatened. The contrast between the two forms of power was clearly made in *The Old Curiosity Shop*; for almost immediately after the description of Little Nell's terrors by night, comes the dialogue between the magistrate and the woman whose son he had transported for theft: Nell merely overhears it and walks away.

Dickens's contempt for the magistracy runs through all the early novels. The Nupkinses and Fangs are the instruments of Government which touch the people most closely, and it is in them that the conception of government held by the ruling class can be most clearly seen. It is an almost entirely negative conception; its end is Public Order, and the only means to the end is 'putting down'. The Whig governments after the Reform Bill had made one or two bold innovations: they had tinkered with Law Reform; but when faced with any crisis they had nothing to offer but the old methods of repression by force and intimidation through the Law. In 1839 armed associations of 'respectable' citizens were spoken of just as they had been in the year of Peterloo. Dickens's criticism of such methods appears plainly in *Martin Chuzzlewit*: in Chapter XXXI, when Mr. Pecksniff has dismissed Tom Pinch, Dickens apostrophizes social duty:

> Oh late-remembered, much-forgotten, mouthing, braggart duty, always owed, and seldom paid in any other coin than punishment and wrath. . . .

He apostrophizes the judge and the bishop, and ends with the magistrate:

> Oh magistrate, so rare a country gentleman and brave a squire, had you no duty to society, before the ricks were blazing and the mob were mad, or did it spring up, armed and booted from the earth, a corps of yeomanry full-grown!

Such duty, that of individuals each working in the limited sphere of their offices, even when carried out with the utmost energy, sense, and goodwill, could still hardly be adequate to the problems of government and organization set up by new conditions in town and country; it is significant that though Dickens found in its neglect one symptom of the failure of the ruling classes, he never once attempted to give one of his benevolent characters any public office; there is no portrait in any of his fiction of a good judge, a good bishop, or a good magistrate: *The Old Curiosity Shop* contains almost the only examples in his early books of a good schoolmaster and a good parish priest. All the books abound with ridiculous minor officials. It certainly is easy, as Bagehot righteously pointed out, to make any kind of government look ridiculous, in any of its instruments, if your only aim is to be funny: but that was not Dickens's only aim. His problem all through his writing life was to find a kind of political and social power, a government, which he could approve; and in the end he failed. He was not a man of great political understanding and vision, not a prophet: his imagination worked on the data society gave him; and at times he clutched even with over-ambitious hope at what he was given.

The outstanding fact in the Early Victorian Age was that the machinery of life designed to control an aristocratic, agricultural, and mercantile society could not control the society that industrial capitalism had imposed upon the older scheme. Dickens, as we have seen, was an exceedingly practical person, who thought in terms of money and getting things done: in other words, he was more concerned with administration than with politics proper. Though so clearly a good member of the middle class, he never exalted the political power of his class. He shared suspicion of the 'mob' with Burke and Brougham; but he never accepted Brougham's specious equation of 'the people' with the middle classes, 'the wealth and intelligence of the country, the glory of the British name'. He was not bamboozled by the Reform Bill of '32 into the belief that as the middle class was so wide the legislation of the new House of Commons would coincide with the interests of the people as a whole: he saw it working, and it most plainly did not. He was left to find the means by which the 'people as a whole' could find expression for its interests.

He was realistic enough to see that no such means of expression could be found unless an adequate system of education lay behind it; but also to see that such a system was scarcely to be achieved in his own time. Yet he was never forced by his despair of 'un peuple éclairé' as immediately likely, into the later Toryism of such people as John Austin and W. R. Greg. In fact he became more sympathetic towards the aims of Chartism after the main Chartist movement, with its physical-force associations, had died away.[1] There is no sign in all his work that he was ever attracted by the despotic doctrines of Carlyle; but the focus of his interest was always rather on administrative than on political problems.

It is only in the 'fifties that Dickens begins to make general attacks on the central administrative departments of Government; and in this, as in so many other things, he was following rather than leading public opinion. His criticism was only possible when 'the standard of administrative efficiency in Great Britain had risen to an extent not realized at the time', when 'the public expected more of its civil servants and departments of state'.[2] The greater expectations on the public's side were a consequence of a changing attitude to centralized administration brought about

---

[1] e.g. in *A Poor Man's Tale of a Patent* (*Household Words*, October 19, 1850).
[2] E. L. Woodward: *The Age of Reform*, p. 255.

largely by the work of Bentham, which had found positive expression in various innovations and reforms since 1832. The typical Briton even in mid-century was still, like Podsnap, suspicious of centralization on traditional grounds: even Buckle[1] seemed to think there was condemnation merely in stating that Government inspectors in France examined fish and weighed loaves of bread; and the last chapter of Mill's *Political Economy* is a classical statement of that guarded jealousy of the central power that has marked all English political thought from the seventeenth century to the beginning of the twentieth. But opinion was shifting, uncertain, and prepared to judge each case on its merits; and hardly anyone was prepared to maintain that the old machinery of government through Lords Lieutenant, Justices, Corporations, Parishes, Manors, and the various bodies of local Commissioners was adequate to an industrialized modern state; yet it is on the whole remarkable that the status and powers of the Poor Law Commissioners were so generally accepted. Much as Dickens hated their work and policy, he never objected in principle to a central Board and unified control; his fear was rather that new Guardian might be old Overseer writ large: his sustained jeering at Vestries and Beadles showed no love of parish autonomy. He claimed to judge administration by its efficiency, not by any theory of powers, and he was remarkably free from the old-fashioned radical prejudice that economy for its own sake should be a leading principle of government; if any responsibility was undertaken money should be spent on it.

He approved the centralized administration of France when he found it worked. The coaches and cabs of Paris were better than those of London:

> But, it is done by Centralisation! somebody shrieks to me from some vestry's topmost height. Then, my good sir,

[1] *History of Civilization*, Chapter IX.

let us have Centralisation. It is a long word, but I am not at all afraid of long words when they represent efficient things. Circumlocution is a long word, but it represents inefficiency; inefficiency in everything. . . .[1]

But equally he damned the centralized administration of England when he thought it failed; and it frequently failed, as in the Crimean war, because though centralized, it was not unified. His knowledge of such business had begun with his knowledge of his father; and the early sight of John Dickens struggling with the accounts of the Navy Pay Office must have been a main cause of his almost neurotic contempt for Departmental methods.

> More obstruction of good things and patronage of bad things, more extravagance, jobbery, ignorance, conceit, saving of cheese-parings and waste of gold, have been committed in these Dockyards (as in everything connected with the misdirection of the Navy), than in every other branch of the public service put together, including even the Woods and Forests. . . . I mean to do all the little I can, to have England governed by men of merit, and not by fine gentlemen . . . no privileged class is, by a direct dispensation of Providence, born to the broad arrow. . . . They may have taken possession of it as a matter of course, but that is another thing. It shows us, the people, the effect of a little combination on their part; and I think it is almost time for us to show *them* the effect of a little combination on ours.[2]

The Graham reforms of 1832 had been a move towards unification at the centre: various independent bodies of Controllers and Commissioners of the Navy had been brought under the more direct control of the Board of Admiralty, and expenses, as usual, were cut. But at the other end much of Dickens's indictment held good till after the Crimean War.

[1] *Railway Dreaming* (*Household Words*, May 10, 1856).
[2] *One Man in a Dockyard* (*Household Words*, Vol. III, p. 557, September 6, 1851).

A few months after his article, for instance, a nauseating scandal occurred in the Royal Clarence Victualling Establishment at Gosport. Nearly 70,000 lb. of preserved meat, 'warranted equal to sample, and to keep sound and consumable for five years', had been in store there for just over a year. This was examined, and only about 7 per cent was found fit for human food. The rest was so foul that the examiners drenched themselves in disinfectant, and often left off work early because of the stench. The canisters contained all kinds of offal and garbage, roots of tongue, pieces of palate, coagulated blood, clots of hair, lumps of gangrenous kidney, pieces of intestine with dung in them, and 'other abominations'.[1] Jobbery and corruption in victualling contracts were common, and ships' pursers lived mainly by commission on the stores they took on board. Such things were made possible largely by the fact that the ordinary seamen were no part of the permanent Navy, which officially consisted only of officers and ships; anything was thought good enough for a rough free-lance whose only status in the service was that he served in a particular ship just so long as it was in commission and was then discharged. He was merely an instrument to be used as hard as possible while it was needed. This system meant, moreover, that in times of crisis ships found it very difficult to raise crews because of the sudden demand. In March 1853 a large part of the fleet was suddenly put into commission as a warning to Russia. Lord Clarence Paget found it quite impossible to fit and man his ship in time to obey orders,[2] and other commanders were kept hanging about in the dockyards, sometimes several hundred men short of their full complement. In spite of these

[1] When a farmer applied to the local authorities to buy the offal for manure, he was told to apply to the Lords of the Admiralty; and meanwhile it was all uselessly dumped in the sea.

[2] *Autobiography*, p. 79.

and many other anomalies the muddles of the Naval administration in the Crimean War were less than those of the Military.

It was, of course, the Crimean campaign that made the Circumlocution Office parts of *Little Dorrit* peculiarly topical, and they were substantially fair. No preponderating blame was ever fastened on any individual;[1] the whole system failed and its members with it. Dickens took up one of the main points that had been made very clear by the war—that division of responsibility between various departments was an effective check upon getting anything done. The division of powers at the top between Secretary of State for War, Secretary at War and Commander-in-Chief was reflected in the absence of any machinery for co-operation between the various parts of the forces in the field. The utter breakdown of the Commissariat and Medical Service, though partly due to sheer ignorance of what the campaign involved, was due more to the cumbrous machinery which seemed to exist only for the purpose of delaying orders. The medical supplies lying unopened on the dock and the cargo of cabbages thrown into the sea were adequate examples of how not to do it.

Dickens himself took no part in the first stage of the political attack on the Government;[2] he only came out into the open when Layard started his public campaign in the summer of 1855. On June 15th Layard's motion for reform throughout the Civil Service had been defeated in the Commons by 359 to 46, and Dickens spoke at the Drury Lane meeting of the Administrative Reform Association on the 27th. His speech itself was of little consequence, but his appearance at the meeting at all and his treatment of

---

[1] The first title of *Little Dorrit* was *Nobody's Fault*.

[2] Roebuck's motion for a Select Committee of Inquiry, which led to the defeat of the Aberdeen ministry and Palmerston's becoming Prime Minister, was made January 29, 1855.

the subject in the novel must be seen in a wider context than that of the war. For some years past the whole question of administrative reform had been widely discussed. The Northcote-Trevelyan report of November 1853 had been made at Gladstone's request, and among his papers was found a private memorandum from a 'leading reformer' which put very clearly the attitude of the Tite Barnacles:

> The existing corps of civil servants do not like the new plan, because the introduction of well-educated, active men, will force them to bestir themselves, and because they cannot hope to get their own ill-educated sons appointed under the new system. *The old-established political families habitually batten on the public patronage*—their sons legitimate and illegitimate, their relatives and dependents of every degree, are provided for by the score.[1]

Carlyle, in 1850, had pushed the whole business forward in the third of his *Latter-Day Pamphlets*, an essay which, cut to a third of its length, would have been funnier and more conclusive than the Circumlocution Office parts of *Little Dorrit*. The Carlyle hero there appears as the super civil servant, a Herculean man, who should come to clean the Augean stables of Downing Street and sweep up the 'mountains of pedant exuviae and obscene owl-droppings' made by the 'dexterous talkers having the honour to be'. The question was whether Hercules could be discovered by open examination according to a syllabus drafted by Dr. Jowett of Balliol: neither Dickens nor Carlyle would say, while Gladstone held to his vision of the sixth-form boys of the public schools recognized at last for what they were, the true aristocracy of England, by a central Board of Examiners.

This aristocracy did not finally come into its own till 1870, the year of Dickens's death: meanwhile

[1] Morley: *Life of Gladstone*, Book IV, Chapter IV, Section 3, and Appendix.

various shifts and changes were made in most departments, and the principle that the administrative grade
should be separated from the clerical came to be
generally accepted. The changes in the War Office
made in the crisis of 1855 were not fundamental, and
four years later Florence Nightingale was still complaining to Sidney Herbert that it was

> a very slow office, an enormously expensive office, a not very
> efficient office, and one in which the minister's intentions can
> be entirely negatived by all his sub-departments, and those
> of each of the sub-departments by every other.[1]

It is strange in all the political discussions of the
Civil Service in these years to see how the question of
efficiency is nearly always treated as secondary to
questions about patronage and the relations of officials
to ministers and to the Crown. In all that was said
and written there is nothing stranger than Henry
Reeve's assumption in the *Edinburgh*[2] that in *Little
Dorrit* Dickens was attacking the 'universal system
of jobbing and favouritism which was introduced into
the public service by Sir Charles Trevelyan and Sir
Stafford Northcote, shortly before the time when Mr.
Dickens began his novel'. It was a great weakness in
Dickens's reply[3] that he did not take this point up,
for it shows how ingrained was the *suspicion* of jobbing and favouritism even in reforms which were
honestly intended to minimize them. What Gladstone
called 'rational confidence in the intelligence and
character of the people' was very difficult indeed so
long as this backstairs atmosphere prevailed. Even
Macaulay, at the very time when he himself was
devising all the details of exams for the I.C.S., said

---

[1] Quoted in *The War Office*, by Hampden Gordon, 1935 (Whitehall Series).

[2] July 1857.

[3] *Household Words*, August 1, 1857. This article is mostly taken up with
pointing out, against Reeve, that the official treatment of Rowland Hill exemplifies
rather than disproves the general condemnation of the Circumlocution Office as
obstructing initiative, merit and efficiency.

of Trevelyan's plans: 'I am afraid that he will pay the examiners too high, and turn the whole thing into a job.'[1]

The ideas behind administrative reform came mainly from Bentham and the Mills, the practical experience mainly from India House, where both the Mills were Civil Servants, or from India itself, where special knowledge was more obviously necessary than in England. Benthamite ideas were re-imported from India by Macaulay and Trevelyan, and then linked again to the home experience of such men as Chadwick and Leonard Horner. If only Macaulay had not been more cautious, conservative, and inactive over English affairs than over Indian; if he had not been content, as Secretary at War and Paymaster-General, to accept inefficient routine with such complaisance; if, in fact, he had not allowed himself to be sterilized by the Whig tradition—the treatment of the administrative problem by the Cabinets of the 'fifties might have been very different. Confused by the bugbear of 'place' (of which the Whigs so well knew the value), by the fear of encroachment on personal and local liberties, and by the ancient cry for economy, the political advocates of mere efficiency were in danger of appearing a pedantic clique. But for once the pedants had a great deal of public feeling on their side, and Dickens was a mouthpiece of it.

He intervened, as usual, in the stylized character of the plain man. It is obvious, in spite of Reeve, that he was attacking the pre-Benthamite, pre-Chadwick, pre-Trevelyan offices rather than the new departments which were beginning to tie their red tape with a difference;[2] and he himself made this clear in the short but almost perfect speech in which he proposed a

---

[1] G. O. Trevelyan: *Life of Macaulay*, Chapter XIII.

[2] His article, *Red Tape*, was chiefly an attack on the absurdities of the Window Tax, which was repealed 1851.

toast to the ill-fated Board of Health which survived only from 1848 to 1854.[1] When he made that speech *Bleak House* was not yet written, and *Household Words* had been running only just over a year: his main work for 'sanitary reform' was not yet begun. Yet he said then that some of the valuable reports of Mr. Chadwick and Dr. Southwood Smith, strengthening and much enlarging his knowledge, had made him earnest in this cause in his own sphere. This seems to point to the fact that the publication of the last part of *Oliver Twist*, including the description of Folly Ditch,[2] closely followed upon the Poor Law Commissioners' Report of 1838 which contained the first detailed official account of public health in London. Chadwick's prodigious report on the whole country followed in 1842,[3] and in 1843 Dickens was in direct touch with Southwood Smith, whom he counted as a friend.

This was Dickens's closest contact with administrators under Bentham's influence, and it affected his view of society and of social problems very deeply. In *Dombey and Son* he first attacks on a wider front: in the earlier novels crime, hypocrisy, cruelty, and the Poor Law were the great evils, and personal kindliness the great good; society was not seen as a whole, though there was evil in all its parts. Good and evil were still mainly private things, to do with a man's own conscience and the effect of his acts on his immediate neighbours. But Public Health could not be dealt with in this individualistic way: one foul cesspool might infect a score of families; the directors of one foul water company might infect a whole town; one man's meat might literally be another man's poison. Quilp dead, and buried in a crowded grave, might in all

[1] Dinner of the Metropolitan Sanitary Association in 1851. The phrase 'fifteen years ago' must have been a slip for thirteen.

[2] See below, p. 217.

[3] *Report . . . from the Poor Law Commissioners, on an Inquiry into the Sanitary Condition of the Labouring Population of Great Britain . . . July 1842.*

innocence ruin more decent folk than Quilp alive could ruin with the utmost exertion of deliberate malice. The plot of *Dombey and Son* suggests the dangerous link between the classes—in the influence of Mrs. Brown and her daughter scheming in the worst of slums on Carker and the Dombeys: but also, at the beginning of Chapter XLVII, of which the main subject is the growing breach between Edith and Dombey, there comes a curiously sudden, inept, and passionate piece of propaganda for Public Health; on the pretext of asking whether Mr. Dombey's master-vice was natural or unnatural, Dickens goes on to ask in general 'what Nature is, and how men work to change her, and whether, in the enforced distortions so produced, it is not natural to be unnatural'.

There follows a long rhetorical homily against the slums, centred on two ideas that run through much of his later work—that the slums are bound to produce stunted barbaric individuals, and that they can infect the whole of society with crime and disease:

> Look round upon the world of odious sights—millions of immortal creatures have no other world on earth—at the lightest mention of which humanity revolts, and dainty delicacy living in the next street, stops her ears, and lisps 'I don't believe it!' Breathe the polluted air, foul with every impurity that is poisonous to health and life; and have every sense, conferred upon our race for its delight and happiness, offended, sickened, and disgusted, and made a channel by which misery and death alone can enter. Vainly attempt to think of any simple plant, or flower, or wholesome weed, that, set in this foetid bed, could have its natural growth, or put its little leaves off to the sun as GOD designed it. And then, calling up some ghastly child, with stunted form and wicked face, hold forth on its unnatural sinfulness, and lament its being, so early, far away from Heaven—but think a little of its having been conceived, and born and bred, in Hell!

The 'redemption' of such a child is the work undertaken by Redlaw at the end of *The Haunted Man* (1848). Later the homily goes on:

> Oh for a good spirit that would take the house-tops off, with a more potent and benignant hand than the lame demon in the tale, and show a Christian people what dark shapes issue from amidst their homes, to swell the retinue of the Destroying Angel as he moves forth among them! For only one night's view of the pale phantoms rising from the scenes of our too-long neglect; and from the thick and sullen air where Vice and Fever propagate together, raining the tremendous social retributions which are ever pouring down, and ever coming thicker! Bright and blest the morning that should rise on such a night: for men, delayed no more by stumbling-blocks of their own making, which are but specks of dust upon the path between them and eternity, would then apply themselves, like creatures of one common origin, owing one duty to the Father of one family, and tending to one common end, to make the world a better place!

The chapter is brought back to Edith and Dombey by saying that on such a morning too they would wake to a knowledge of the world around them, of their own relation to it, and of a 'perversion of nature in their own contracted sympathies and estimates'. All this is, of course, ludicrously detached from the theme and mood of the novel: but it is a preparatory sketch for one of the main strands of the plot of *Bleak House*; for there disease engendered in the filth of Tom-all-Alone's, besides killing off several children, ruins Esther's face and is apparently also the cause of Lady Dedlock's death. The series of chances that links Jo to the lives of the wealthy characters is intended as an imaginative expression of the idea of solidarity between the classes. Tom-all-Alone's is the moral type of a London slum, rather than a carefully documented portrait based on the evidence of reports,[1] but it is described in a frenzy of bitterness, impatience, and anger. As things are going in the 'fifties 'Tom only may and can, or shall and will, be reclaimed according to somebody's theory but nobody's practice. And in the hopeful meantime, Tom goes to perdition head foremost in his old determined spirit.' And Dickens continues with the idea that he contains a destroying fate for the upper classes:

> But he has his revenge. . . . There is not an atom of Tom's slime, not a cubic inch of any pestilential gas in which he lives, not one obscenity or degradation about him, not an ignorance, not a wickedness, not a brutality of his committing, but shall work its retribution, through every order of society, up to the proudest of the proud and to the highest of the high. Verily, what with tainting, plundering, and spoiling, Tom has his revenge.

Written in the short interval between two national epidemics of cholera, that of 1849 and that of 1854, this may appear too plainly an appeal to self-interested fear. But fear was no longer popular or normal in the upper and middle classes as it had been in the early 'forties, and Dickens amid growing complacency becomes more passionate. Nobody's theory will do; it must be practice. But what practice does *Bleak House* offer? It offers nothing but the personal ministrations of the 'good doctor', Allan Woodcourt, and his pockmarked wife, backed by the geniality of Mr. Jarndyce.[2]

---

[1] There is no need to repeat again here the awful details of bad water, bad drainage, bad ventilation, and overcrowding collected in every town throughout the country; they are best read in the reports themselves; the worst are collected by Engels; there are excellent summaries by Mr. and Mrs. Hammond in *The Town Labourer* and *The Age of the Chartists*, and by Mr. R. H. Mottram in *Early Victorian England*, where also a few brilliant paragraphs by Mr. Young lead up to 'the drinking water brown with faecal particles, the corpses kept unburied for a fortnight in a festering London August; mortified limbs quivering with maggots; courts where not a weed would grow, and sleeping-dens afloat with sewerage'.

[2] Charles Kingsley, in *Two Years Ago* (1857), described the attempts of an active doctor to introduce the Nuisances Removal Act and the Public Health Act into a Cornish fishing-town when cholera was threatened in 1854. Tom Thurnall is an interesting contrast to Allan Woodcourt.

But this tame solution, in keeping with his general method in the novels, does not represent his whole opinion about the matter. His speeches and journalism in the 'fifties are more and more filled with the question of Public Health[1] and are concerned with the immediate problem of whether his aims can be achieved through the working of the Public Health Act of 1848 and the General Board of Health set up by it.

His speech in proposing a toast to the Board was made in surroundings which pointed the contrast between prosperity and misery with painful and typical irony:

> On Saturday evening last [i.e. May 10th, 1851] the Metropolitan Sanitary Association and the friends of sanitary reform held their first public festival at Gore House, Kensington, under the auspices of M. Soyer, who, for the first time, threw open his *Symposium* for the entertainment of a public body. The banquet was laid out in the Baronial Hall, which was elegantly fitted up for the occasion. The walls were hung with a number of paintings, the productions of Madame Soyer. Behind the chairman was a trophy emblematical of the grand banquet supplied by M. Soyer, at York, to his Royal Highness Prince Albert, and the mayors of the different English cities and boroughs. Chinese lanterns, suspended from the ceiling, diffused a mellow and pleasant light over the brilliant pageant below; and the tables were decorated with a profusion of plate, rare exotics in vases, and silvered mirror globes which multiplied and reflected the brilliant scene. A military band was in attendance, but concealed from the view of the spectators; and the gallery at the end of the hall was filled with ladies.[2]

Lustrous globes, moreover, hung from the lanterns,

---

[1] Hardly a number of *Household Words* is without some mention of it, and there are frequent series of linked articles over several months. Its monthly news-supplement, *The Household Narrative*, had as the regular heading to a section of its contents: 'Social, Sanitary and Municipal Progress'.

[2] *Illustrated London News*, Vol. 18, p. 417. The brilliant scene is depicted on the following page.

pedestals about the room, supporting statues and enormous urns, sprung from incredibly decorated pilasters, while the two hundred gentlemen of the company peered at each other round tall epergnes of fruit crowned with pineapples. In this setting the Chairman, Lord Carlisle, explained that the average deaths from preventable disease in England were 50,000 a year, 'outstripping in numbers the carnage of the most destructive campaigns and the most protracted wars', and that in some districts half the children born died before the age of five. The statement that these deaths threatened 'especially those who fill the many walks of humble life' was greeted with 'Loud Cheers', and the chairman went on to hope that M. Soyer 'besides exercising those more recondite mysteries which qualify him to take his place with Vatel, Ude, and Carême, should communicate to our English kitchens some of those arts which would render them at once more cheap and more versatile than they have hitherto been'.

It is difficult to imagine how Dickens's words, which read so sensibly and simply, must have sounded in such an atmosphere: it is not so difficult to imagine his conscious delight in saying there that 'the furious pestilence raging in St. Giles's no mortal list of lady patronesses can keep out of Almack's', and that the use he had made of his eyes and nose had only 'strengthened the conviction that certain sanitary reforms must precede all other social remedies, and that neither education nor religion can do anything useful until the way has been paved for their ministrations by cleanliness and decency'. This conviction clearly underlies much of his work in the 'fifties; and he was equally sincere in his support of the Board of Health, at least so long as his friend Carlisle, as Commissioner of Woods and Forests, was a member of it.

But the very fact that he *was* a member of it raised

again the question of 'powers'; for he was not a departmental head responsible to Parliament. Membership
was a Crown appointment and the Board had, within
the limits of the Act, unchecked administrative
authority. The two other original members were
Ashley and Chadwick as paid member and Secretary:
Southwood Smith was soon added as a second paid
member. Thus on the old cry of 'Centralization!'
followed the other of 'Jobbery!' The Board maintained, according to some local authorities, 'a system
which is productive of benefit to those alone who are
appointed to carry it out'. Even while cholera was still
raging in '49 the Guardians of St. James's, Clerkenwell,
refused to appoint two doctors nominated by the Board
as house-to-house visitors because they 'thought this
most unusual proceeding on the part of a government
board seemed so much like jobbing'.[1] It was made out
that house-to-house visiting was either in principle
wrong, or, if right, begun too late: one suspicious local
doctor announced: 'If this system does not manufacture
cases of cholera and diarrhoea, I shall be indeed sur-
prised!'; and a clerk to Guardians stated that its 'sole
object is to afford employment to a large number of
medical men at the expense of a credulous public'.[2]
So came the third cry of 'Extravagance!' Had not
Parliament voted the Board the enormous sum of
fourteen thousand pounds, and could they still pretend
that delays occurred in a crisis because they could not
get their 'machinery' into operation? Behind all this
was the awkward fact that Southwood Smith, Grainger,
Sutherland, and the other medical advisers to the Board
knew a great deal more about cholera than the local
doctors who resented their intrusions: it was claimed
against them, for instance, that rice-water diarrhoea

[1] Letter of James Bennett, Assistant-Clerk to the Board of Guardians, to *The Times*, dated September 22, 1849.
[2] Letter of Bennett to *The Justice of the Peace*, dated September 26, 1849.

was not even a premonitory symptom; but it is in fact the first stage of cholera itself.

The Board had to deal with this epidemic in the first year of its life, and it worked consistently for the adoption of preventive measures—cleaning of streets, removal of nuisances, burning of infected clothing, whitewashing of house-walls, and so on: but not even Chadwick could force his way, without fuller compulsory powers from Parliament, through the chaotic jungle of vestries, paving board and sewage commissions whose help was needed before the central board could begin to act or even advise on what action might be taken.[1] 'My vestry,' said Dickens, in his speech, 'even took upon itself to deny the existence of cholera as a weak invention of the enemy, and that denial had little or no effect in staying the progress of the disease. We can now contrast what centralization is as represented by a few noisy and interested gentlemen, and what centralization is when worked out by a body combining business habits, sound medical and social knowledge, and an earnest sympathy with the sufferings of the working classes.'[2] But the constitution of the Board was in fact weak: it worked under a compromise between permissive and compulsory legislation; it cast the irritating shadow of bureaucracy without possessing its best effective substance. Neither Chadwick nor Ashley had the temperament to overcome these defects and to encourage the formation of local Boards of Health by tactful conciliation. When the general Board was abolished in 1854, though 182 local boards had been set up, they covered only two millions of the population; and *The Times*, which had supported the General

[1] 'In the parish of St. Pancras . . . there are no less than 16 separate paving boards, acting under 29 acts of parliament, which would require to be consulted before an opinion could be safely pronounced as to what might be practicable to do for the effectual cleansing of the parish as a whole.' *Report by the General Board of Health . . . up to 1849.*

[2] cf. *Our Vestry* (*Household Words*, Saturday, August 28, 1852).

Board in its struggles of 1849 decided that 'we prefer to take our chance of cholera and the rest, than to be bullied into health'.[1]

But Dickens did not let Chadwick and the others drop so easily. During the autumn of 1854 he published in *Household Words* a series of articles[2] on Public Health designed to rally opinion behind an active central power. 'A Board of Health,' he wrote in the first of them, 'can do much, but not near enough. Funds are wanted, and great powers are wanted; powers to over-ride little interests for the general good; powers to coerce the ignorant, obstinate, and slothful, and to punish all who, by any infraction of necessary laws, imperil the public health.' Lord Seymour, who had been largely responsible for killing the 1848 Board in Parliament, was trounced for 'cutting jokes' about cholera. In the second article Seymour was attacked again; Sir William Molesworth was attacked for not introducing the Public Health Act into Portsmouth in circumstances where the Act itself required it;[3] the inaction of the Newcastle authorities, which Ashley had used at length in his defence of the original Board, was made virtually equivalent to murder. The former Board of Health, the new Board, and the Registrar-General were called the three very best helpers in the war against disease that the public hitherto had had, but 'equipped with funds and powers miserably scanty'.

[1] See J. L. & B. Hammond: *Lord Shaftesbury*, Chapter XII.

[2] (a) *To Working Men*, October 7, was by Dickens himself. Of (b) *A Home Question*, November 11, he wrote to Macready on November 1: 'It is not written by me, but is generally of my suggesting.' (c) *Commission and Omission*, November 18, was not by him. The articles appeared while Mrs. Gaskell's *North and South* was running as a serial.

[3] i.e. when the death-rate in any district exceeded 23 per 1,000. The article says that the Act rightly recognized the policy that it could not be introduced in any place where a majority of the inhabitants were against it; but this seems to be a very doubtful interpretation of what was to be done in special circumstances under Sect. 10. The Act had also said that local Boards of Health were to be formed on the petition of 10 per cent of the inhabitants: this was afterwards attacked as giving discontented or factious minorities an improper chance of going behind the backs of the local authorities.

Both articles implied that it was useless to look for an increase of centralized power in any policy sponsored by Parliament alone, and appealed direct to the working classes to force the hand of Government by protesting unanswerably against the conditions in which they had to live. 'The whole powerful middle class of this country,' said Dickens, 'newly smitten with a sense of self-reproach—far more potent with it, we fully believe, than the lower motives of self-defence and fear—is ready to join them.' The points of a new People's Charter—of Public Health—were sketched out; but how its programme was to be put forward without either votes or violence, or what benefit the moral support of the enfranchised classes might be when they had failed by their votes, was not made clear. In fact, these emotional middle-class appeals to the masses show how hard it was for the opinion and sentiment behind Dickens's practical aims to find expression through existing political forms, or for them to be made even intelligible to the existing parties. Vested interests and mere conservative prejudice were too strong on the one hand, while on the other a few doctrinaire radicals like Bright gave a false colour of reason to an obstructionist case. Parliamentary divisions on public health followed no party lines; the association of Ashley with Chadwick, and Dickens's own approval of the man who had rigged the Poor Law were no more anomalous than what happened in the lobbies. These well-meant attempts to cut in behind the whole existing political machine were doomed to failure unless they were accompanied by the demand for the organization of the working classes for political and social action of every kind; and that demand Dickens was not ready to make.

It is also curious that such very various people as Dickens, Ashley, Chadwick, and Joseph Hume should have agreed to underestimate, not to say ignore, the possibility of regenerated local government. These *Household Words* articles and also that called *Commission and Omission*, which dealt with the sewerage of Greater London, all praised the work of Dr. Simon in the City, where a vigorous medical officer co-operating with the local authorities had already achieved a great deal. But such co-operation was certainly exceptional, and Dickens's hatred of 'vestrylization' prevented him from thinking generally in terms of collective localized power.

There was also a strong authoritarian strain in him which has often been overlooked.[1] In an age of predominantly individualistic thinking, when the individualist case plainly breaks down, as over Public Health, a man of passion and feeling is likely to rush to the opposite extreme, and to assume that highly concentrated central power is the only cure. For Carlyle, competitive individualism had universally failed and had to be universally overridden; but he was highly individualistic in his conception of the overriding power: the hero was in effect just the man who had won the competition: individualism was self-destructive in its own terms. Dickens's search for an overriding power only began when he was convinced that individualism had failed in a particular case; and the power he sought, being limited to that case, had no predetermined form. He was inclined to accept what offered, and to delight in the mere fact that it was power of a kind. This helps to explain his almost fanatical devotion to the Metropolitan Police.

[1] e.g. by Mr. G. M. Young: 'Dickens's ideal England was not very far from Robert Owen's. But it was to be built by some magic of goodwill overriding the egoism of progress; not by law, and most emphatically not by logic. . . . In all Dickens's work there is a confusion of mind which reflects the perplexity of his time; equally ready to denounce on the grounds of humanity all who left things alone, and on the grounds of liberty all who tried to make them better' (*Early Victorian England*, II, pp. 455–6). This is on the whole true of the novels, less true of the short stories, and hardly true at all of the occasional journalism and speeches. The difference of attitude in the different types of writing does certainly reflect perplexity. There was a strong authoritarian strain in Robert Owen's socialism.

In all his stories and articles about the police there is scarcely a breath of criticism. His arrangements with Wills to make night-tours of the gas-lit station houses; the detectives' party in the office of *Household Words*; the trip down the river in the Thames police launch—show well enough his inquisitively morbid interest in all forms of crime and death; but they show too a kind of clerical satisfaction in the functioning of a well-run organization. There is some hint of this in Inspector Bucket; it is clearer in the police-office parts of *Our Mutual Friend*; and clearer still in some of his articles:

> The Detective Force organized since the establishment of the existing Police, is so well chosen and trained, proceeds so systematically and quietly, does its business in such a workmanlike manner, and is always so calmly and steadily engaged in the service of the public, that the public really do not know enough of it, to know a tithe of its usefulness.[1]

After the river expedition in *Down with the Tide*:

> We looked over the charge books, admirably kept, and found the prevention so good that there were not five hundred entries (including drunken and disorderly) in a whole year.

Policemanlike too was his admiration of the working of Ashley's Common Lodging-House Act of 1851, which gave powers of inspection to the police themselves, and in practice encouraged an almost military discipline in the houses for single men; which was a strange conclusion for those earlier praises of the poor man's humble hearth.

This authoritarian attitude developed partly from political difficulties, but was also partly due to personal characteristics in Dickens himself. There are many reasons for believing that he belonged to the Freudian

[1] *The Detective Police* (*Household Words*, July 27, 1850. Vol. I, p. 409).

'anal type', obsessed with neatness and precision. He was a dandy in his clothes; he was pernickety about being punctual; his writing-desk was, according to a host of proud witnesses, always in apple-pie order; when he gave village-sports at Gad's Hill he reported with peculiar glee that the spectators kept in line along the course and that nobody got drunk; he would personally supervise the minutest details of stage carpentry for his plays; one local opinion of him near Rochester was that he was 'masterful'. Such a character frequently has an intense interest in its opposite. The dandy was the student of the shabby-genteel; the exact man created Mr. Micawber and Mr. Dick; the over-tidy householder gloried in the jumble of the curiosity shop and Traddles's chambers. So too the social reformer spent much more time describing Deputy Chaff-Wax, the Exchequer tally-sticks, and the tying of tape than the reports, case-books, and ledgers of the Board of Health. But the obvious delight in disorder has tended to obscure an underlying cause of it—the natural preoccupation with order. He loved to describe the muddle he hated.

In all this work of the early 'fifties the idea of muddle is spreading over wider and wider social fields. *Hard Times* came out between April and August 1854, and Stephen Blackpool's reiterated comment, ''Tis a' a muddle' is superficially the least hopeful moral to be got from any novel Dickens wrote. Discussion of the book has often centred too much on Macaulay's condemnation of it as 'sullen socialism', and the almost exaggerated praise that Ruskin gave it in *Unto this Last*; for it is the least read of the novels and probably also the least enjoyed by those who read it. Even Mr. Edwin Pugh called it 'dry', 'hard', and 'the least alluring' of them all. The most common general explanation of the book's failure is that Dickens was writing of people and things quite outside the range of his own experience. This is, in itself, of course, no explanation at all, or *A Tale of Two Cities* would stand equally condemned; but the decision to write just when he did about industrial Lancashire with no more experience than deliberate copy-hunting could give him was peculiar in several ways. The fashion for industrial novels was already passing: *Martin Armstrong, Helen Fleetwood, Sybil, Mary Barton,* and forgotten stories by such people as Camilla Toulmin, belong to the late 'thirties and 'forties, the period of Chartism, terrific unemployment and angry strikes. The experience and motives behind their authors were very various. Mrs. Trollope, who had to write for money and had made her name with social criticism, found a topical subject and approached it with an average sense of decency and justice; Mrs. Tonna was inspired by her evangelical faith to a hatred of the factory system and its child employment even more passionate than Ashley's; Disraeli was caught for a moment by an image of feudalism and found his experience in official reports; Mrs. Gaskell lived every day among the things she wrote of, and only discovered her talent because she thought the experience had to be used.

It has often been said that Dickens was a good deal influenced by *Mary Barton* in writing *Hard Times*: it might even be added that he was influenced by Elizabeth Gaskell herself[1]—it is impossible that he should have known her without being half in love—for his editorial letters about her work show an affectionate care abnormal even for him. But there was never any question of a conscious and deliberate imitation of her, or of Carlyle, or of anybody else. The strange thing is that though most readers find *Hard Times* dry and brain-spun, Dickens said of it himself that he had not meant to write a new story for a year, when the

---

[1] From his letter of April 21, 1854, it is plain that he had talked over the story with her in some detail when he was in the North.

idea laid hold of him by the throat in a very violent manner.

What this central idea was there is no means of knowing; but it is plain that *Hard Times* is one of Dickens's most thought-about books. One of the reasons why, in the 'fifties, his novels begin to show a greater complication of plot than before, is that he was intending to use them as a vehicle of more concentrated sociological argument. All his journalism shows too that he was *thinking* much more about social problems, whereas earlier he had been content to feel mainly, and to record a thought, when it occurred, in emotional dress. The objection to such a character as Gradgrind is not just that he is a burlesque and an exaggeration —so are Squeers and Pecksniff—but rather that in him the satire is directed against a kind of thought: he is in fact the only major Dickens character who is meant to be an 'intellectual': 'His character was not unkind, all things considered; it might have been a very kind one indeed if he had only made some round mistake in the arithmetic that balanced it, years ago.' Dickens was caught with the idea of a man living by a certain philosophy, as in the past he had often been caught with the idea of a man living by a master vice such as miserhood or hypocrisy or pride. Such vices he understood, but he did not understand enough of any philosophy even to be able to guy it successfully. But he obviously felt during the 'fifties, when Public Health and Administrative Reform were keeping him so closely to social-political problems, that there must be some essential flaw in the reasoning of such a man as Bright. The creation of Gradgrind is an attempt to track it down. The despondent atmosphere of the whole book reflects the failure to do so.

This atmosphere is concentrated in Stephen Blackpool. In him Dickens tried to rescue the idea of personality in an individual industrial worker. Stephen's successive defeats by the Law, by the Trade Union, and by his employer might have become the material of genuine tragedy, if Dickens had been prepared to accept his death from the beginning as inevitable and unanswerable; but he was hankering all the time after a way to avoid the proper tragic solution, and the result is nothing but a slow record of inglorious misery and defeat. Dickens did not want to admit that Stephen's bargaining power—whether against Bounderby, his marriage, or life itself—was negligible, but wrote as if there might be an unexpected solution at every turn. There is no difficulty about Stephen's relation to the Law or about his relation to Bounderby;[1] the true crux is in the part of the plot that deals with the Trade Union, and in making it so Dickens was apparently trying to work out, in the actual writing of the book, the implications of his old ideal of *man to man* benevolence in the relations between employers and labour in large-scale industry. Three points were emphasized in the treatment of the Union—Stephen's inexplicable obstinacy in refusing to join it; Dickens's hatred of Slackbridge; and the difference of mood and attitude of the other workers towards Stephen as men and as Union members under Slackbridge's influence.

For the Union meeting itself he did a thing which was very rare for him—he deliberately went in search of copy, to Preston, to watch the effects of a strike of the cotton workers there which had dragged on for weeks.

---

[1] Ruskin's judgement that Bounderby was merely a 'dramatic monster, instead of a characteristic example of a worldly master' is probably more or less true if we assume Coketown to be Manchester and Bounderby a man of the local prominence that Dickens gives him. But if Coketown was some smaller place, a monster of that kind might well have got such power over its life. Mr. and Mrs. Hammond have, for instance, found a possible original (*Town Labourer*, p. 302): 'P——d, the Beggar-maker, who sits on the destinies of the Poor, we have made a Man of him, whose Mother hawked about the Streets a small Basket; on two Spinners being deputed to ask for a small advance of Price, had the audacity to thrust one of them from him with an Umbrella and discharged them both' (Letter from Committee of Manchester Weavers, 1823, *Home Office Papers*, 40, p. 18). Such a man might well have grown into Bounderby by the 'fifties.

He seems to have gone expecting to find discontent, disorder, and even rioting, and his first impression caused surprise and a sort of sentimental gladness that everything was so quiet and the men generally so well-behaved. When he came to write up the visit for the article *On Strike* in *Household Words* (Feb. 11, 1854) there was overlaid upon this first impression a certain horror at the idleness. He seemed to be asking whether these were perhaps after all the lazy poor, in whose existence he had never believed. The article describes the two meetings of the strikers that he attended, and they are obviously the foundation for the Union meeting in *Hard Times*: it stresses their order and courtesy, the efficiency of the business and the competence of the men's local leaders; it decries the influence of an outside orator who is a prototype of Slackbridge; it makes clear that the men fully believed in the justice of their case, but that, at the same time, they had no hatred or resentment for most of the employers: it does, however, quote one example of a threatening notice against a particular man, together with various other placards and verses: the moral approval seems to be all on the side of the strikers. But the political conclusion is not that the strike is right:

> In any aspect in which it can be viewed, this strike and lock-out is a deplorable calamity. In its waste of time, in its waste of a great people's energy, in its waste of wages, in its waste of wealth that seeks to be employed, in its encroachment on the means of many thousands who are laboring from day to day, in the gulf of separation it hourly deepens between those whose interests must be understood to be identical or must be destroyed, it is a great national affliction. But, at this pass, anger is of no use, starving out is of no use—for what will that do, five years hence, but overshadow all the mills in England with the growth of a bitter remembrance?—political economy is a mere skeleton unless it has a little human covering and filling out, a little human bloom upon it, and a little human warmth in it.

The only practical suggestion is that the dispute should be submitted immediately to impartial arbitrators agreed upon by both sides. This paragraph is extremely important and interesting, because in it Dickens accepts the fundamental ethical and political proposition of the political economy he generally so much deplores. The interests of employers and employed must be assumed to be identical or must be destroyed. The doctrine of the identity of interests was common to the utilitarians and the economists: on the question of *theory* there is no real difference between Dickens and W. R. Greg:[1] he is not in the least a Socialist.

This paragraph also helps to explain why the satire of Mr. Gradgrind is comparatively ineffective; for Dickens is not even intending to attack the whole philosophy which he thought was represented in the Manchester men; he is only attacking the excessive emphasis on statistics; in fact he is repeating Mr. Filer over again, and he seems to have no uneasiness about whether such satire is adequate or important. He is through all these years, however, extremely uneasy in his attempts to find a channel through which the desires and needs of an ordinary decent working man like Blackpool can find expression. Why, when he recognized the capacity of such men for conducting their own business, did he reject the Trade Union solution, and reject it as emphatically as a Manchester man like Greg?

On the whole the 'Combinations' of the 'thirties and 'forties, whether organized locally, by trades, or nationally, had avowed revolutionary aims. The extent

---

[1] See especially Greg's long review of *Mary Barton*, of 1849, reprinted in *Mistaken Aims and Attainable Ideals of the Artizan Class* (1876), and his *English Socialism*, of 1850. Both essays are directed against the impatient philanthropy of 'feeling' as compared with the long-distance philanthropy of the economists. The cures for labour disputes are that the working class should be more provident and should, by the study of political economy, realize the necessary identity of their interests with those of the employers.

to which their members advocated the use of physical force was less important than the fact that they were widely believed to do so; but, physical force aside, they were revolutionary in the sense that they did not accept the doctrine of the natural identity of interests between Capital and Labour, and were in their political activities more or less conscious of a class-struggle; and this consciousness was shared by their opponents. The Chartist failure of '48 meant widespread disillusionment in the possibilities of working-class political action, and the reviving unions of the 'fifties concentrated more on the immediate problem of collective bargaining within particular trades than on the formation of huge amalgamations with political aims.[1] Dickens seems to have realized that this change was happening, but he shared two common popular misconceptions about it; the first was that the leaders of such unions were bound to be demagogic frauds like Gruffshaw and Slackbridge; and the second was that the unions were likely to violate liberty by being exclusive and tyrannical towards workers who refused to join them:[2] both points were heavily underlined in *Hard Times*. The first of these objections was a legacy from the earlier amalgamating, revolutionary period, and was very largely justified. For in the period of Chartism and the large national unions the working-class movement was grotesquely top-heavy and therefore unstable: the middle-class mistrust of 'demagogues' and 'paid agitators', whatever its motives may have been, was justified in the sense that national leadership had not developed out of solidly organized cells of local opinion. Local organization

[1] The Amalgamated Society of Engineers, for instance, was founded in 1851, and played a very important part in the development of Unionism in the next twenty years.

[2] Even Kingsley, when calling himself a Socialist, wrote to a Manchester friend, March 28, 1856: 'I admire your boldness in lifting up your voice to expose the tyranny of "Union" Strikes. From my own experience of demagogues . . . I can well believe every word you say as to the "humbug" connected with the inner working of them.'

even in the 'fifties was likely, as in the Preston strike, to be an *ad hoc* affair called into being by a particular dispute; and Dickens was faithful in his reporting, in *On Strike*, of the way that outside influence was likely to be overridden: but in *Hard Times* he regarded local opinion as dynamically inferior to Slackbridge's bluster: he meant to imply that Stephen was socially boycotted in spite of a predominating feeling in his favour, and the other workers bamboozled out of their better selves; and he made the distortion seem more serious by giving Stephen no better reason for not joining them than a mysterious promise. The objection to unions on the ground of exclusiveness and tyranny followed inevitably from the general misunderstanding of their nature: Dickens realized that when Stephen had been both boycotted by his fellow-workers and sacked by Bounderby he had no chance of getting another job; but he did not draw from this the conclusion that an individual worker *cannot* be the equal of an employer in bargaining power, and that the ideal bargaining for labour-price talked of by the economists only had any meaning when the bargaining was done by a unanimous combination. His emotional admiration for the conscientious blackleg was not based on any alternative argument. But he did not abandon all hope of finding some means other than the unions by which such men as Stephen might be politically and socially articulate; he was still groping after it later in the year in the address *To Working Men* and the other articles on Public Health we have already discussed.

However, the failure of *Hard Times* in two main strands of its plot and in so many of its major characters does not lessen the force of the mixture of fascination and repulsion that Dickens felt for the industrial scene in which the book was set. The fascination, which appears in the descriptions of the night railway journey out from Coketown to Bounderby's house, of the people surging to the mills in the morning, and returning at night to their various homes, has the interest in life and movement, which is plain everywhere in his work, heightened by greater speed and tension. The repulsion is generally more marked, as it is in the Black Country parts of *The Old Curiosity Shop*; the dismal appearance of the competing chapels, the rigidity of the Bounderby bank and the grim business discipline which intrudes on every detail even of domestic life, express once more the Southerner's dismay at what he could not assimilate; but underlying it there is unresting indignation at the impoverishment of human life that such things implied. This indignation is not crude and immature anger, but rather a disturbed mood that colours every perception, contributing a great deal to the unpopularity of *Hard Times*. The book is ultimately unsatisfying and oddly uncomfortable to nearly all its readers; but this very fact is the main thing that has to be considered in assessing its value as a novel; unanswerable disquiet was normal among the very few who were not misled into the easy optimism in which Bagehot typifies the 'fifties; Ruskin's exaggerated praise of *Hard Times* may be understood as a recognition that a work of art, by conveying this at least to others, might make up for many other imperfections; and even those writers whose economics and social criticism were more solid and thoughtful than Dickens's betray in their own ways shifting of opinion and misplacement of emphasis—Mill, Ruskin, and Arnold are examples—which equally, express the practical embarrassment of the time.

.   .   .   .   .

These details show Dickens's political problems in the 'fifties, the decade in which he was most concerned with politics, on which his work and his 'creed' must be judged. Though in the revolutionary period he had seen 'the necessity of a mighty change', his impatience increased as the danger of violence receded. Impatience such as his is a common characteristic of reformers with no taste for the business and organization of politics: it disqualified him even from editing a political newspaper with the immediate policy of which he agreed. An impatient reformer who wants a short-cut to a tolerable world without the risk of violence is always in a weak political position; and the consciousness of his relative impotence is likely to lead him to screaming and jeering where he might argue. At times Dickens's political work is tedious for this reason: he repeats his old jokes and jibes as if the structure of humbug would collapse under the weight of mere monotony. But in his best work—as for a humane and constructive Poor Law and for Public Health—when his impatience is backed by solid argument it acquires a special political importance, for it is directed against the barriers between public opinion and the executive. These barriers were of two main kinds: (1) the degrading business of Parliamentary elections and political graft in general, (2) the sinister interests of sections of society.

Dickens did not attack either of these kinds of obstruction purely in economic terms or class terms: he always regarded 'sinister' interests as a question of personal morality, not as the inevitable consequence of the existing social and economic structure. He saw clearly enough that such interests multiplied and spread with the growth of capitalist prosperity—his bitterest attack on economic power is in his last completed book; but he never disputes the principle of individual right to any kind of property; his aim is to restrict, either by moral conversion or by law, its abuse.

Many writers since Dicey have seen in Dickens's work a development from individualistic political ideas towards some kind of collectivism; but it is an easy mistake to attribute to him a more positive conception of a collectivist society than he ever had. We have seen how under the pressure of events and opinion in the 'fifties he came to accept state interference, and in certain instances to agitate angrily for its extension: but there is no reason to suppose that there was any fundamental change, even if unconscious, in his political and social aims. In his acceptance of the forms of executive power he was opportunist almost to the point of irresponsibility: the only guiding principle behind this opportunism was his personal belief that what he advocated coincided with the desires and needs of all decent and disinterested men. There was no dramatic and significant transformation of a sentimental bourgeois individualist, praising all the go-ahead family virtues, into an efficient analyst of bourgeois culture working to supplant the whole scheme of life that had conditioned his own success; nor was there any important change in the direction or character of his sympathies. But from some time in the later 'forties there was a definite growth in his vision of society from the merely personal and domestic towards an understanding of the complicated interaction of countless social forces.

The long-standing dispute about whether Dickens was a 'democrat' or not has often been too much detached from the circumstances in which his political work was done, and the details of it. Forster, for instance, added in comment upon the Birmingham declaration of faith: 'It may be suspected, with some confidence, that the construction of his real meaning was not far wrong which assumed it as the condition precedent to his illimitable faith, that the people, even with the big P, should be "governed". It was his constant complaint that, being much in want of government, they had only sham governors.' This has often been taken as an authoritative anti-democratic statement from one supposed to know: but Dickens's actual work gives scarcely any hints about what he believed to be the proper origin of efficient executive power: disregarding all political machinery he appealed now to 'the public', now to working men, now to Mr. Bull, now to men of goodwill, identifying in each case his own views with public opinion, and the public with those to whom he appealed.

It is important that the last novel he wrote in the 'fifties should have been *A Tale of Two Cities*, for it is the only one that has politics as a central theme. The main impression it leaves on its readers (and it is usually read very young) is of the horror and bloodiness of the revolutionary atmosphere, and the grim idea of Vengeance epitomized in Madame Defarge. There in the most melodramatic form is an idea of the Terror taken over by many from Burke; but its place in the scheme of Dickens's work is with the mob in *The Old Curiosity Shop* and the Gordon Riots. But in spite of the obvious hatred that Dickens has for the mad and uncontrollable fury of the mob, he uses the description of it to express, or to work off, something of his own neurotic impatience and anger. He danced and slaughtered with the crowd.

A plain thesis can be extracted from the book: the aristocrats deserved all they got, but the passions engendered in the people by misery and starvation replaced one set of oppressors by another. One aristocrat can be rescued to repent and live in the decent quietude of England; one individual can assert his goodness against the double evil of the rest. But the concentration of emotion is never on Charles Darnay; it is all on the wild frenzy of people who have committed everything to violence. Dickens hated and feared such violence; there is not a sign of approval or defence of it; he attributes every kind of monstrous wickedness to its leaders; but he projects into his treatment of it his own feelings of desperate impotence in the face of the problem of political power.

CONCLUSION

NO discussion of Dickens's books as historical documents can avoid considering the quality of his reporting and the modifications of his 'facts' by reticence, by exaggeration, and by the peculiar working of his eye interpreting the 'facts' in the very moment of seeing. This book has deliberately treated him as if he were a journalist more than a creative artist; and he was in fact a journalist of the finest kind. There is no such thing as pure reporting; even a hack has to find news, and then can only see it in the schematization of his own mind and only send it to his editor in his own style; he can only depersonalize it into commonplace, and commonplace derives its quality from journalism and not from events. Modifications in reporting are more or less deliberate, and in interpreting journalism it is best to deal with the more obviously deliberate modifications first.

There is one such modification in Dickens which stands out above any other—his reticence about what he thought might be offensive. In the preface that he later added to *Oliver Twist* he said that he had aimed to describe the dregs of life '*so long as their speech did not offend the ear*'. And he applied this principle to many things besides the conversations of Sikes and Nancy; everything was written with an eye on decency, and he himself worked by the rule he mocked at in Podsnap, that there should be nothing in his books unfit for a Young Person. His doing so was almost universally approved: critic after critic praised his 'purity' right up to the end of the century. Even Frederic Harrison could write in 1895:

Here is a writer who is realistic, if ever any writer was,

in the sense of having closely observed the lowest strata of city life, who has drawn the most miserable outcasts, the most abandoned men and women in the dregs of society, who has invented many dreadful scenes of passion, lust, seduction, and debauchery; and yet in forty works and more you will not find a page which a mother need withhold from her grown daughter.

[*Studies in Early Victorian Literature*, p. 143.]

And he adds that every word was written *virginibus puerisque*. This constant censorship that Dickens imposed upon his work can partly be explained by the common practice in Victorian society, in all classes, of reading books and periodicals aloud in the family circle; he had children always in mind. But such an explanation does not go nearly far enough; for he does not merely omit incidents and words and phrases that might be put in, but conceives his whole plot in a way that underestimates the brutality, squalor, and filth of the setting in which it is supposed to develop. Consider, for instance, the part played by Nancy in *Oliver Twist*. She is supposed to be a thorough-going whore who is working full-time for Fagin and Sikes: one of her jobs is to keep her eye on the apprentice thieves, and apparently also to recruit for the gang. So far she is historically all right: but how in fact would a girl be used in such work? A witness before the Mendicity Society put it like this:

I have known as many as forty or fifty regular prostitutes and thieves lying hicklety-picklety in one lodging-house, and many of them from different towns. They tell one another all they know. Bad wenches enticing young lads from home to these houses make more thieves than ought else.

and

The lodging-house people try to get young girls from the factories to sleep there, which is a sure way of making their house.

Nancy's job would certainly have been to use her sex as much as possible with boys like Charley Bates and the Dodger; and the whole atmosphere in which Oliver lived in London would have been drenched in sex; but Dickens does not even obscurely hint at such a thing. The same is true of the life of Good Mrs. Brown and her daughter in *Dombey and Son*, and of their hold over Rob the Grinder.

The censorship touches also many other sides of Dickens's reformist writing. His descriptions of the filth of the slums are quite inadequate to the truth; when Oliver first goes to Saffron Hill the Great, for instance, he says that 'the air was impregnated with filthy odours' and that 'drunken men and women were positively wallowing in filth', and so fails to make it clear that the street was full of the emptyings of pots and privies.[1] Even Tom-all-Alone's is not described in its full horror. The account of Jacob's Island and Folly Ditch towards the end of *Oliver Twist* is less outspoken than that of the same place in Kingsley's *Alton Locke*. None of Dickens's degraded drunkards—such as the hero of *The Drunkard's Death* in the *Sketches* or Mr. Dolls in *Our Mutual Friend*—approach the facts about the kind of drunkenness he was meaning to describe. Neither he nor Kingsley would have given details of the cancer of the scrotum (George II's sweeper died of it) that was the peculiar and horrible disease of climbing boys, nor explained how the boys were often let down privies through the seat 'for the purpose of fetching watches and such things'.

In trying to interpret this kind of reticence—often thought of as 'Victorian prudery'—the distinction has

---

[1] There is an interesting example of purely verbal reticence on this point in Mrs. Gaskell's *Mary Barton*, Chapter VI: 'Women from their doors tossed household slops of *every* description into the gutter; they ran into the next pool, which overflowed and stagnated. Heaps of ashes were the stepping-stones, on which the passer-by, who cared in the least for cleanliness, took care not to put his foot.' The reader is left to make a plain inference about what the ash-piles were.

to be kept in mind between reticence in speech and reticence in idea. Was there a real unwillingness to admit and understand the implications of the facts, or merely an unwillingness to mention them? If both, how did they interact? Of the verbal reticence there is an interesting example in Engels's *Conditions of the Working Classes*: he at least cannot be accused of unwillingness to face the worst; and he was no Victorian, as his book was written in German and not translated for many years. Yet after describing conditions in a common lodging-house he says: 'Thefts are arranged and things done which our language, grown more humane than our deeds, refuses to record.'[1] The *Quarterly Review*, which was by far the most plain-spoken of the Victorian journals on sanitation, said in March 1843 that some of the details given by Dr. Alison and Dr. Cowen about the wynds of Glasgow were 'too offensive to be transcribed'. The growth of such reticence in Europe in the first half of the nine-teenth century—it was by no means confined to England —was a very curious social symptom. The cultivation of niceness, delicacy, and 'refinement' was partly the reflection in manners of the Rousseauistic emphasis on sentiment in literature; but in England at least it was also a protective blind against some of the worst evils that industrial society was generating. The absurd position was thus reached that the very people who were anxious to expose and correct the evils felt them-selves muzzled by a convention to which the evils themselves had given rise. Dickens himself said that 'dainty delicacy living in the next street' stopped her ears and refused to believe in the squalor of the slums that he was attacking, but yet he felt under the con-straint of writing in terms by which her delicacy would

[1] English Trans. 1892, p. 31. The 1845 Leipzig edition reads: 'es werden Diebstahle verabredet oder Dinge getrieben, deren Bestialität unsere menschlicher gewordenen Sprachen nicht in Worten wiedergeben wollen.'

not be offended. The increase of consciousness that the foul things were foul meant also an increase both in the wish to turn away from them and in the wish to cure them; but the cure could only come about if they were exposed in their full foulness, about which dainty delicacy did not like to hear. So there was an extremely vicious circle—a circle from which Dickens never quite escaped.

He did not escape in his language (which was studiously modified even when his indignation was greatest); but he did not escape in his ideas either. In much of his description of what he considered to be the grosser kind of social evil there seems to be a contest between a frank acceptance of it as an unwelcome fact and the desire to minimize it because it was unwelcome. There is an open sincerity in his manner when he is attacking injustice, cruelty, humbug, and so on, which is lacking when he attacks the cruder consequences in sex, drink, and dirt, of bad social conditions. It is this perhaps more than anything that stamps him with the morality of a middle, an ambiguous, class. There is, for instance, a tremendous human reality in the drunkenness of J. D. Burn's stepfather,[1] which that of Dickens's drunkards lacks; it was observed directly by a working-class child and no later education could pervert the vision, though a sententious layer of morality was imposed upon it. In Bamford's autobiography there is an acceptance of the fact that one of his childhood women-friends had gone on the streets in Manchester,[2] which is far more moving than Dickens's tears over Martha. And towards the other end of the social scale of writers, the brutalization of the people in Disraeli's Wodgate is more apparent than that of those in Dickens's St. Giles's. In class and habits of feeling Dickens was too far removed from such things to assimilate them fully (he was ashamed when he

[1] *The Autobiography of a Beggar-Boy*, Anon., 1855, the earlier chapters.
[2] *Early Days*, 1849, Chapter XX.

thought he had become a manual worker), but not removed enough to treat them with detachment. The process of censorship which made him conceal for years the proletarian episode in his own boyhood was similar to that which was constantly at work in his fiction.

This whole question has an important bearing on another side of his work. One of the problems with which he was concerned in one way or another in nearly all his novels was the influence of environment, especially in childhood, upon habits and character. The emphasis of the argumentative and exclamatory part of his reformist writing is upon the fact that environment matters more than anything. He points to the filthy soil of the slums and asks how you can expect anything but weeds to grow there; he sees the treatment of the children in workhouses and concludes that they will never escape the crippling stigma of pauperism. The point of his work for sanitary reform was that even education and religion are no good till people have more light, more air, more room, clean houses, clean streets, and decent water. In education the system of Miss Monflathers produces a useless snob; that of the Grinders a crook.

But the belief in the inevitability of these consequences is not borne out in the plots of his stories. The most notable example is, of course, that of Oliver Twist. Up to his first rescue by Mr. Brownlow, Oliver's whole experience of life was such as could only make him either a monster or a wretch; and the purpose of that part of the book is to show that he was bound to be. But he is not. Two things are in conflict—the desire to show the immense damage that such an environment and upbringing can do, and the desire to demonstrate that the fundamental goodness of human nature can survive almost anything. It is perhaps unnecessary to emphasize the contribution of Oliver's gentle birth to this result; because a similar thing, on a smaller scale, happens to poor Jo whose parents were not genteel. The spark of goodness was kept glowing in him by Hawdon and Snagsby, and was fanned at last to a tiny flame by Allan. Nearly all modern readers find these conclusions thoroughly unconvincing; and they could not have seemed convincing even to contemporaries if the full horror and grossness of the life that such children must have lived had been displayed. The censorship is thus closely linked to the course of the story that Dickens wanted to tell.

It is not an adequate explanation of such contradictions to say that the convention of the happy ending was so firmly established that Dickens felt compelled to conform to it against his better judgement:[1] the conflict was in himself.

Less need be said about the other main way in which he modified the 'facts'. After every book he wrote he was solemnly assailed for 'exaggeration' on some point or other; and of course exaggeration was essential to his whole method. It was not consciously exercised: he did not see something and then say, 'I must exaggerate that'. The exaggeration was already in the seeing. Examples in earlier chapters compared with historical details of the same kind—about workhouse food, Government offices, the obstructionism of parish authorities, and so on—show a more deliberate kind of exaggeration than there is in the creation of such people as Mrs. Gamp; but the minutely telling details upon which the effect depends (as 'an onion twice a week, and half a roll on Sundays') are always made in the most practical terms, and run parallel to the factual 'truth'. The exaggerated components are in the same medium as the thing that is being exaggerated; and from this the created world gets its great solidity. Dickens's fiction is far more effective as propaganda in practical things—Poor Law, Health, Administration—

---

[1] The ending he certainly altered for this reason was that of *Dombey*: Walter Gay was to have been a failure.

than in its satire of types of character. For the most effective satire of a vice in fiction is one from which the reader recognizes its symptoms in himself. Occasionally Dickens succeeded in this way (Pip's snobbery, for instance, comes home); but in general his method precluded that kind of self-criticism. His satirical portraits are enjoyed just because they make it easy to say that here are the symptoms betrayed by somebody else. Nobody can ever, when reading about Pecksniff, Podsnap, or Sapsea, have said with heartfelt and torturing humility: 'How true! it's me': but readers have so readily attached the labels Pecksniff and Podsnap to others that they have added new words to the language. Dickens used to tell with great glee how one day Mrs. Nickleby in the flesh protested to him that there never could be such a person as Mrs. Nickleby: but the story reflected as much on his own method, thinking of him as a moralist, as on the lady's perception.

There is not the slightest doubt that his general moods of kindliness and indignation, meeting, as they did, a need of the time, deeply influenced the emotional attitude of thousands of people to social problems, particularly during the 'forties. 'There have been at work among us,' said one Nonconformist preacher, 'three great social agencies: the London City Mission; the novels of Mr. Dickens; the cholera.'[1] But if we come to ask whether any specific piece of legislation or any particular reform was directly due to his work the answer must be, No.[2] In all practical matters his ideas ran alongside those of people more closely connected with practical things; he did not initiate, and in his major campaigns he did not succeed. For the most impressive thing about 'Reform' between 1832 and 1870

---

[1] Quoted by Mr. G. M. Young: *Early Victorian England*, II, p. 460.

[2] The example most commonly quoted to show that he did have some immediate effect is that of his letters to the *Daily News* on public executions in 1846, in which he described the crowd at the execution of two murderers called Manning. But even so, public execution was not abolished till 1868.

was its sloth. No genuine attempt to meet his objections to the Poor Law was made till the appointment of the Royal Commission of 1905. Private persons were still imprisoned for debts over £20 until 1861, and imprisonment for debt was not formally abolished before 1869. Effective compulsion on local authorities about Public Health only began in 1866 after still another epidemic of cholera, and the Local Government Board was only set up in the year after Dickens's death. The Civil Service was thoroughly reorganized only in 1870, and the foundations of a national system of education were delayed till the same year. In the face of these facts it is clear that the immediate effect of Dickens's work was negligible.

The growing class of administrative 'experts' was as little susceptible as the political oligarchy to the kind of appeal he was making; and later in his career the political press, which had on the whole in earlier years respected his motives and methods even when it disagreed with his aims, began to turn against the whole idea of propagandist fiction. By the mid-'sixties the *Westminster* had become the staid mouthpiece of a rather conservative kind of Liberalism; and it gave a very superior sneer at *Our Mutual Friend*:

> True art has nothing to do with such ephemeral and local affairs as Poor Laws and Poor Law Boards . . . a novel is not the place for discussions on the Poor Law. If Mr. Dickens has anything to say about the Poor Law, let him say it in a pamphlet, or go into Parliament. Who is to separate in a novel fiction from fact, romance from reality? If Mr. Dickens knows anything of human nature, he must know that the practical English mind is, as a rule, repelled by any advocacy in the shape of fiction. And to attempt to alter the Poor Law by a novel is about as absurd as it would be to call out the militia to stop the cattle disease.
>
> [April 1866.]

Bagehot went so far as to say that in his later books

Dickens spoke 'in a tone of objection to the necessary constitution of human society'. Such judgements, as we have seen, were a consequence of the increase of prosperity in the mid-century and of complaisance. But it is interesting to see that this also produced a view of the proper sphere of fiction, which had little or no currency in the 'thirties and 'forties; there was a growing desire to detach novels from sociological controversy; George Eliot's typical problems were those of the intellectual and emotional adjustment of individuals to society; and *Edwin Drood* is the most mellow and private of Dickens's books.

But his adherence to fiction as a means of propaganda for thirty years had revolutionized the attitude of the common reader to novels. Carlyle's strictures on novel-reading in the *Essay on Scott* became finally irrelevant when Dickens's reputation had been established. He touched areas of the reading public that scarcely any other non-religious writer reached; and beneath the few thousand sophisticated people who quickly reacted to changes of taste he kept alive the idea that novels could be something more than dope. He is still the only one of the great English novelists who is read at all widely among simple people. Many people maintain that this is largely because his reformist sentiment is valuable as a permanent statement that it is the goodness of individuals in society that matters more than its institutions and forms. But goodness itself is relative; its moods and qualities change. The particular forms of his goodness were conditioned by his time; and it seems more likely that he is now read and will go on being read because he made out of Victorian England a complete world, with a life and vigour and idiom of its own, quite unlike any other world there has ever been.

INDEX

225

226

INDEX